Gardening
in Retirement
Bernard Salt

Acknowledgements

I offer my thanks to the following for their contribution to the production of this book.

Garden Answers magazine and photographer Colin Leftly, for almost half the photographs.

My brother, Len Salt (30 years Head Gardener at Birmingham Botanical Gardens), for checking the manuscript.

My friend, Keith Thompson, for the demonstrations on pages 71 and 144.

Fuji Film Company, for supplying film.

Defenders, for the photographs of biological control organisms, on pages 124 and 126.

Colegrave Seeds, for the lower photograph on page 68.

Peta (UK) Ltd, for the photographs on page 5.

Traditional Garden Supply, for the photograph on page 135.

The various items and varieties mentioned in this book are not endorsed by the publishers.

© 2001 Bernard Salt
Published by Age Concern England
1268 London Road
London SW16 4ER

First published 2001

Editor   Gillian Clarke
Production   Vinnette Marshall
Designed and typeset by GreenGate Publishing Services, Tonbridge, Kent
Printed and bound in Great Britain by Bell & Bain Ltd, Glasgow
Illustrations by Bernard Salt, unless stated otherwise above
Cover photographs by Colin Leftly

A catalogue record for this book is available from the British Library.

ISBN   0–86242–311–2

Bulk orders

Age Concern England is pleased to offer customised editions of all its titles to UK companies, institutions or other organisations wishing to make a bulk purchase. For further information, please contact the Publishing Department at the address on this page. Tel: 020 8765 7200. Fax: 020 8765 7211. E-mail: books@ace.org.uk.

Contents

Preface

When you retire, a whole new world opens – no forced routine, no travel to work, no costs of work and your time is your own. Life really begins with a new set of challenges and additional rewards. Now is the time for that first greenhouse – to replan the garden – to raise your own plants instead of buying them – to grow some of your own food – and to get involved with the local garden club. Or possibly now is the time to adjust your garden to give maximum pleasure with the minimum of effort. There may be more holidays and extra weekend breaks that will leave your garden unattended.

The boundary between organic and non-organic gardening is rather blurred. I have covered both methods with an emphasis on the organic. With few exceptions, the photographs were taken in my garden, developed by Ivy and me during the eight years since our retirement.

The weather in these islands is varied: when do we sow those seeds or plant that tender subject? Any timings stated in this book are for the Midlands; these will be somewhat late for parts of the south and west and a little early for the north, east and higher altitudes.

Sadly, the garden, once a source of great pleasure, may become a chore and burden. There is so much to do to maintain it in its former glory that we may even consider moving to a home with a very small garden.

I have attempted to address all these aspirations and problems and trust that the advice given will aid a happy retirement.

Bernard Salt
Corner Farm
Walton on Trent
Swadlincote DE12 8LR
e-mail: bernard@cornerfarm.demon.co.uk

About the Author

Bernard Salt has spent a lifetime working with the soil and has sixty years' experience to draw upon. His varied and successful career has included ten years farming in Wales, twenty-six years teaching gardening in a large Staffordshire comprehensive school and eight years as a garden writer and journalist.

His school garden was chosen by the late Geoff Hamilton for a full length *Gardeners' World* programme on BBC2.

His three previous gardening books have all been reprinted and he has three regular features in *Garden Answers* magazine. He answers the 'Reader Enquiries' in the *Kitchen Garden* magazine and produces its 'Letters' page in addition to regular features and articles. More recently he has become involved with the internet, writing web pages for gardening365.com and a daily e-mail tip to its surfers.

Ten years ago Bernard moved to Derbyshire where he, together with his wife Ivy, have developed a unique organic garden from scratch. This one-acre garden covers the full spectrum of gardening and has special features such as a dry bog. The garden is in regular use by photographers shooting material for books, magazines and the internet. With few exceptions the 300 photographs in *Gardening in Retirement* were taken in Bernard's own garden.

Bernard has developed new ways of growing plants and maintaining a delightful and productive garden without a lot of physical effort. This wealth of knowledge and experience lies between these covers.

Chapter 1

Caring for the Gardener and the Soil

Health and safety

The last thing you want to do in the garden is get hurt. Attention to design and a few simple precautions will ensure that your garden is a safe place to be. The first thing to do is make sure that your tetanus vaccination is up to date. My doctor tells me that the vaccine remains effective for ten years – better check when you last had yours. It is important to be sure that you are protected – the tetanus bacterium lives in the soil and can enter your body through a scratch.

Electricity

Lights and power points in the garden, garden shed and greenhouse should all be fitted by a qualified electrician.

All electrical items should be connected to the mains through a residual current device (RCD). This disconnects the supply of electricity if a fault occurs (eg accidentally cutting through a cable).

It is important that all outside fittings are officially approved for that purpose.

Water

Outside taps must by law be fitted with a non-return valve to stop water from re-entering the mains. Where this is not an integral part of the tap, a valve must be fitted between the tap and the hose.

Chemicals

A few common-sense measures are necessary for the safe use of chemicals:

- Read the instructions before using them.
- Always wear gloves when handling chemicals.
- When spraying, wear a mask and goggles.
- Use chemicals only for their intended purpose.
- Keep chemicals locked away and out of the reach of children.
- Keep chemicals in their original containers and **never** transfer them to other receptacles.

Always take advantage of manufacturers' safety devices. This battery-powered lawn mower will not operate when this plug is removed. This simple precaution could save a child (or adult) from a nasty accident.

Even a very dilute amount of hormone weed-killer will create havoc with garden plants. If you use chemical weed-killers, buy a separate watering can, mark it very distinctly and use it only for that purpose.

Carrying garden tools on your shoulder is a very dangerous practice. The business end is at head height and might hurt someone nearby. Store tools out of harm's way in a rack (see p 142). When you are working with a rake, never lie it on the ground, even briefly. Always lean it against a wall, tree or some such with the head uppermost and the teeth pointing inwards.

This may look a bit extreme but every year garden forks are involved in over 2000 accidents that require hospital treatment.

The top of a garden cane can cause nasty injuries, including damaging an eye. Old film cases make excellent cane caps – better than the bought ones. Simply cut a cross in the lid and force it onto the top of the cane.

Carrying a fork in a safer way.

Before adjusting or examining garden machinery, unplug electric ones and remove the spark plug lead from petrol-driven ones.

Broken glass can make an accident much worse than it would otherwise be. Use plastic cloches rather than glass ones. Glazing a greenhouse with safety glass, rather than standard horticultural glass, may one day prevent an injury as well as the need to replace broken glass.

When selecting materials for path surfaces, the possibility of slipping should be one of your considerations. Some types of concrete slabs become treacherous when covered with wet algae. Keep them algae-free with Armillatox or other algaecide. Ice on paths is dangerous for people of all ages; keeping a container of rock salt for early morning use is a prudent measure that could prevent a painful injury. Be careful, though, when you apply rock salt, as seepage or spillage onto the lawn or planted areas can damage the plants.

Have safety in mind when you are changing aspects of garden design. Steps can be both difficult and dangerous for older visitors but so can sloping paths. Where steps are unavoidable, consider fitting a handrail or support posts that serve the same purpose.

Garden design should also avoid the need for ladders. Where hedges are included, aim to keep them to a minimum height. Even Leylandii *hedges can be kept small by regular trimming. If you have a high-reach pruner, you may not need a ladder – especially if the pruning is done at least once a year. Fruit pickers on long poles are also available.*

Where designs include top fruit (fruit that grows on trees), select your trees with care. Grow bush apples rather than standards. Select other trees on dwarfing root stocks, so that the various operations do not include the use of a ladder (see p 89).

Tools

By the time we reach retirement we all have our favourite tools. The gardening tools needed vary from garden to garden and from gardener to gardener. Most gardeners need fewer than a dozen of

the hundred-plus tools available.

Several tools are self-sharpening, and a well-worn spade or fork is much easier to use than a new one. Others, such as the Dutch hoe and the lawn edger, become blunt and need sharpening with a file now and again – a sharp tool does a better job and is easier to use than a blunt one.

Increasing age may bring increasing aches and pains – bending and gripping may become difficult. These problems do not reduce the joy of gardening but they do make it more difficult. Before deciding to change a favourite tool, see if it can be adapted to your new situation. Special handles are available that are easily fitted to existing tools. A thick handle is easier to grip than a thin one: you can wrap foam rubber round the present handle and hold it in place with electrician's tape. (Make the grip just thick enough so your thumb and index finger begin to overlap.) The weight of a tool becomes increasingly important, so you might like to consider aluminium. An aluminium spade is much lighter than the usual steel one with a wooden handle –

and surprisingly cheap. Beware of novel tools that are heavily advertised: these tend to be expensive and may prove to be unsuitable for your requirements.

Gardening with loss of grip

- Two hands are better than one; use tools designed for two hands wherever possible.

- Select small, light tools.

- Increase the size of handles by covering them with foam and taping it in position.

- Use ratchet secateurs or, if you find these difficult, prune with a very small pair of loppers.

- Select tools that have been designed with special grips.

- Arm grips and handles that bolt onto standard tools are available and can be adjusted to your own particular need.

- Select tools with moulded handles.

- Buy a smaller watering can.

- Use a trolley (see p 59) instead of a wheelbarrow.

- Slip bicycle handlebar grips over your favourite hand tools.

- Use Velcro plant ties instead of string.

Gardening if you have a physical problem

Gardening with a back problem

- Select long-handled tools that can be used without bending.

- Use a kneeler with side supports to grip when getting down or up (see p 56).

- Have long (but light) handles fitted to your existing tools.

- Grow plants that climb (eg sweet peas and runner beans) where some of the tending can be done in a standing position.

- Use cut-and-hold pruners to prevent prunings from falling onto the ground.

This seed sower has adjustable outlet holes and is ideal if you find it difficult to handle small seeds.

Gardening with knee problems

- Use a very thick kneeler – or tape two together.

- A border fork makes a very useful aid when you are rising from a kneeling position.

Soil care

We cannot choose our soil, and have to make the most of whatever type happens to be in our garden. A little understanding will help you to maintain and improve its fertility.

Understanding soil

Soil is basic to gardening. A good gardener keeps the soil healthy and teeming with life. A well-managed soil is essential for a successful garden. There are clay soils, loam soils, chalk soils, silt soils, fen soils, acid soils, alkaline soils, mineral soils, organic soils and mixtures of all of them. No two soils are exactly the same.

Soil consists of tiny particles of crushed rock. Large particles are sand, very small particles are clay. The difference between sand and clay is similar to the difference between grains of wheat and flour. In addition to rock particles, soil contains water, air, mineral salts, humus (decayed organic matter) and organisms, large and small – millions of them in every spadeful.

Adding to this complexity a soil may be acid, neutral or alkaline, measured on a pH scale. In spite of the complexity of soil, its management is easy. All you need to do is cure any waterlogging, keep the soil well supplied with decaying organic matter, control acidity and keep off it when it is wet. When soil dirties your shoes, you are causing damage to its structure!

Two words that often get confused are 'texture' and 'structure'. The *texture* of a soil refers to the size of the rock particles it contains. The *structure* of a soil refers to the way in which these particles are bonded into crumbs. Little can be done to change the texture of a soil but the structure depends upon your skill as gardener. Soil with a pH around 6.5 (slightly acid) that receives regular dressings of organic matter and is not trampled will develop an excellent structure. It will hold the optimum amount of air and water, forming an ideal environment for plant roots.

Sandy soils are described as 'light' because they are easy to work, and clay soils are described as 'heavy'. The best kind of soil is a loam. Loam soils have a mixture of sand and clay particles. Whatever your soil, the way to improve it is the same: regular dressings of organic matter and a dressing of lime ('liming') as necessary. (Test the amount of lime required by using a kit available from most garden centres. You only need to test your soil one year in three.) Liming is more important on clay soil, because it helps to break up the clay as well as reducing its acidity.

Digging

Regular digging is unnecessary. However, an initial deep dig of the area intended for planting is essential when your garden is first laid out.

Digging leaves a bare surface, buries weeds, increases the air content, improves drainage and creates conditions where a *tilth* (crumbly soil on the surface) can be formed. Soil should be dug when it is moist but not wet. Working on a wet soil will do more harm than good.

Years of digging or tramping on the soil may have created a hard, compacted layer of soil just below the depth of cultivation. This compacted layer is known as a 'pan'. A pan impedes both root development and drainage. Once the pan is broken, you can arrange your gardening operations to prevent it from ever forming again. In order to break the pan, you must dig to a depth of two 'spits' (twice the length of the spade blade).

Rotavate or dig?

A light garden rotavator with rapidly spinning blades will not work the soil deeply enough to break a pan. The heavier rotavators, with slow-turning blades, may do the job but they are hard work if you do not use them properly. The trick is to hold the handles down until the blades are at the required depth and then get forward movement by raising the handles slightly. If you hire a rotavator, get one with a reverse gear, as it is well worth any extra hire charge.

Making it easier

Dig to the full depth of the spade but take a small slice of soil – less than the width of the spade.

Do a little at a time and don't feel that you have to dig the whole plot in one go.

Do not turn the soil over when 'forking' the bottom of the trench. Insert the fork to its full depth and pull the handle backwards. This will break the pan. Work your way along the trench, repeating the forking every few centimetres.

Digging an area of soil to a depth of two spits

1 Dig a trench across one end of the area and, using a wheelbarrow, take the soil to the other end.
2 Skim off the weeds along the next row to be dug and place them in the trench.
3 Dig a second trench by turning the soil, spadeful by spadeful, into the first trench. Each time, push the spade to its full depth.
4 Stand in the trench and use a garden fork to dig the bottom of the trench. Work backwards to prevent consolidating the soil.

5 Repeat this process (steps 2 to 4) until the end of the area is reached.
6 Use the soil from the wheelbarrow to fill the last trench.

When you have finished digging, it is best to leave the soil to settle for two weeks or so before planting. If you are inexperienced, the soil may be uneven, but this is unimportant as it can be raked level after it has settled.

Soil care in the flower border

After the initial digging and planting, the soil remains undisturbed except for removing and adding plants. The less you are on the soil the better, especially when the ground is wet. If you have to be on wet soil, place a board on the ground to stand on. This will spread your weight and protect the soil structure.

An annual mulch of decayed manure, garden compost or other organic matter will keep the plants fed and the soil in good heart. Cover any bare soil with a 5–7 cm (2–3 in) layer of mulch. Spraying dilute seaweed extract onto the leaves (a foliar spray) in spring will make good any deficiencies in trace elements and improve the health and vigour of your plants. Take care! Do not spray open flowers, as the petals could stain. There should be no need for additional fertilisers.

Borders of annuals, and other areas that are regularly replanted, can be difficult to mulch. The best plan is to fork manure into the top 10 cm (4 in) of soil immediately after you have pulled up plants that have finished flowering.

The soil by a hedge becomes dry and infertile. You can reduce this effect on nearby plants by preventing hedge roots from competing with them. Turn a number of old compost bags inside out, and dig a trench alongside the hedge. Place the bags on the vertical face of the trench and replace the soil. You need do this only once, as the benefits last indefinitely.

Soil care in the vegetable area

In the kitchen garden use raised beds, separated by paths. The beds need to be 120 cm (4 ft) wide with 60 cm (2 ft) paths between. Beds can be any length but I find that beds longer than 3 m (10 ft) can be tiresome when you have to move several times from one side to the other during an operation. The paths are rather narrow but quite wide enough. A wooden surround increases bed depth and prevents soil from spilling onto the paths. It also forms an anchor on which to staple various plastics. Before setting up beds you should work the soil as deeply as possible. Dig over the area and fork the bottom of the trench after each row of digging. Take care not to bring any sub-soil onto the surface. Manure or other organic matter should be mixed with the soil at the rate of 5.2 kg per sq m (10 lb/sq yd) as digging proceeds.

Line the inside of the wood with black plastic (old compost bags, etc) to protect plant roots from the preservative. ▼

After digging, mark out the beds with string. Shovel the top 15 cm (6 in) of soil from the paths to the beds. Fix the wooden surrounds and never step on the beds again. There is also no need ever to dig again! The type of wood you use to surround the beds depends on what is available in your area: timber from a reclamation yard is one possibility, scaffold planks that have failed safety tests is another. If you live in or near to a farming area, sawn fence rails will be available at an agricultural merchant. If all else fails, two or three tile laths nailed together are suitable. Short lengths of tile laths make ideal pegs to hold the timber surrounds. Some of the materials mentioned will have been treated with preservative. Before fixing the surrounds, give any untreated wood a liberal dressing of creosote.

The trodden soil between the beds will form a path, especially if it is sandy and free draining. If your soil is clay, the path will become sticky when wet; a layer of footpath gravel, spread to a depth of 5 cm (2 in) and raked level, soon consolidates to give you a clean, hard surface. Keep your paths weed-free with an annual application of Pathclear or sodium chlorate, as hoeing disturbs the surface and spoils the path. Be careful not to let sodium chlorate seep into planted areas, as this can damage your plants.

Making it easier

Traditionally, regular digging has been associated with vegetable growing. You can grow more and better vegetables without the need for regular digging. One initial dig and reorganising the area into raised beds makes vegetable growing a very pleasant and rewarding hobby.

Benefits of raised beds

- Very little physical effort is required.
- Kind to your back.
- Almost no digging.
- Higher yields.
- Greater rooting depth.
- Plants can be grown closer together.
- No soil compaction.
- Fewer weeds.
- Crop rotation is easier and more effective.
- Easy to sow a small area at a time, to provide succession.
- Operations can be carried out regardless of soil conditions.
- Pest control is easier.
- The area always looks tidy and well organised.

A problem with narrow paths is that plants such as potatoes soon cover them. Garden canes with horizontal strings tied between is the best way to prevent this.

Feeding the soil

Most soils tend to become acid over time. For maximum yields the acid measurement (pH) needs to be between 6.0 and 7.0. Use a garden centre testing kit every three years and lime the soil if the pH measurement is below 6.0. The kit gives details of amounts needed. The best time to lime is after a crop has been removed. Spread ground limestone over the surface and lightly rake it into the top 5 cm (2 in). Manuring at the same time is not advisable; spread organic matter on the surface two months later.

The soil in a vegetable garden has to work very hard, and you must manure it regularly. Manure is the life blood of the soil – it holds the water reserve, keeps the soil 'open', makes it crumbly, feeds millions of soil creatures and supplies the plants with nutrients. Lucky gardeners have friends with horses, chickens or even cattle; others are not so lucky and have to rely on composting every bit of organic matter they can get their hands on. Fresh manure should be composted for at least six months before using it. If you are short of manure, do not spread it thinly but use it where it will do most good – on 'hungry' crops such as leeks and runner beans.

Add manure by spreading it over the surface after the last crop is removed. The earthworms will pull the manure into the soil, their burrows will aerate the soil and their casts improve its fertility. Any manure remaining on the surface at sowing time is simply pushed aside. Some gardeners prefer to fork manure into the top few inches of soil – working from the paths, of course. An annual dressing will keep the soil fertile and maintain a good soil structure.

How much manure to add?

This is a difficult question to answer, as the weight of manure varies according to how wet it is. A good dressing consists of 5.4 kg per sq m (10 lb/sq yd) of manure that is moist without being wet. This amount is needed every year to maintain humus levels and increase the amount of water the soil will hold.

October-sown grazing rye being covered in spring. This will kill the rye, which can then be lightly forked into the soil.

If you are short of manure or garden compost, an alternative is a 'green manure' crop – a crop grown purely to dig it into the ground. If your soil is likely to remain bare for a few weeks during the growing season, or for several months during winter, a green manure crop is worthwhile.

The green manure crop:

- holds nitrates in the surface layer, which would otherwise be leached away;

- protects the soil structure from damage by heavy rain;

- helps to keep the area weed-free;

- increases the number and diversity of soil fauna;

- maintains humus levels;

- improves soil structure.

Moreover, if the crop is a legume (eg tares or lupins) it also increases the soil's nitrate content.

The seeds for green manure crops are traditionally scattered (*broadcast*) and raked in. It is better to sow in rows, the width of a hoe apart, as this facilitates weed control. There is no need to dig the green manure into the soil. Cover it with black plastic four or five weeks before you intend to plant the next crop. Lack of light kills the green manure and the earthworms begin to incorporate it with the soil.

Almost any quick-growing crop plant can be used as green manure. Suitable legumes include crimson clover, field beans, lupins, trefoil and winter tares. Other suitable crops include, buckwheat, fenugreek, mustard, phacelia and grazing rye (the cereal, not rye grass). I find grazing rye to be the most successful, especially if it has to stand the winter.

Wind breaks

Cold winds seriously reduce plant growth. If your garden is very windy, a wind break on the side of the prevailing wind will help. A hedge is ideal but, where this is not possible, do consider a plastic wind break – available in the larger garden centres. Solid wind breaks (eg a fence) do not work, because they cause eddy currents on the sheltered side. To be effective, a wind break must allow some wind to pass through.

Crop rotation and soil-borne pests and diseases

Pests such as potato eelworm and diseases such as clubroot live in the soil. Fortunately, these problems affect only certain crops – if the crop is not grown, the pest or disease eventually dies out. The art is to prevent a build-up of these problems in the first place. This is done by crop rotation. Crop rotation is quite difficult in a small area such as an allotment – even if you clean your tools between one area and the next, soil is carried on your boots and barrow wheels. The best way to organise crop rotation is to work on a system of raised beds. The soil on a raised bed is never walked on nor subjected to the barrow wheel.

A four-year rotation is probably ideal but very difficult to organise in the kitchen garden, because so many of our crops are brassicas. A three-year rotation is easy and quite effective in controlling most soil-borne pests and diseases.

Three-year crop rotation

Divide the plot into three areas of equal size. Organise the crops into the following groups:

Group 1	Group 2	Group 3
Beans	Cabbages	Carrots
Leeks	Cauliflower	Parsnips
Lettuces	Brussels	Beetroot
Onions	sprouts	Potatoes
Peas	Calabrese	Tomatoes
Celery	(broccoli)	
	Radishes	
	Swedes	
	Turnips	
	Chinese	
	cabbage	

The groups should be planted in the order:

	Plot 1	Plot 2	Plot 3
Year 1	Group 1	Group 2	Group 3
Year 2	Group 3	Group 1	Group 2
Year 3	Group 2	Group 3	Group 1

Chapter 2

Greenhouses, Conservatories and Windowsills

Retirement is an ideal time to buy a greenhouse. It is also the time to make good use of your existing greenhouse.

Choosing a greenhouse

Size is very important. Whatever the size of your greenhouse, there will be times when it will not be large enough. The most popular size is 180 cm (6 ft) wide and 240 cm (8 ft) long. A path down the middle will be 60 cm (2 ft) wide, which allows 60 cm (2 ft) either side for the plants. A much better arrangement is a greenhouse that is 240 cm (8 ft) wide. The path will then have 90 cm (3 ft) either side – giving more plant space from the same dimensions.

Before you buy a greenhouse, it will pay to do some research. Examine the greenhouses on display in DIY stores, garden centres and garden shows. Look at friends' greenhouses and send for brochures from advertisements in garden magazines. Pay particular attention to the height at the eaves, the ventilators and the door mechanism. A wooden greenhouse looks better than a plain aluminium one; whether it also looks better than a green aluminium one is debatable. Aluminium is the better choice as it has many advantages, freedom from maintenance being the most important.

When your greenhouse is in use, it is the plants that are seen, not the frame.

Aluminium greenhouses vary a good deal in quality. The aluminium glazing bars consist of 'T' sections in cheap greenhouses and 'H' sections in the better ones. If your site is windy, a very cheap aluminium greenhouse is not advisable.

Safety is an important consideration. Plastic may not be as attractive as glass but is much safer, especially if grandchildren are likely to be running around. An alternative is to glaze with toughened safety glass. A sliding door is preferable to a hinged one, as it does not catch the wind and can be used as a variable vent. Most greenhouses have a step or a runner across the doorway; these are very easy to trip over, so their height is an important safety consideration.

This Keder greenhouse is 3 m (10 ft) wide and 4 m (13 ft) long. It is clad with an extremely tough plastic, strong enough to bear the weight of several people. The plastic has a life of well over 10 years.

A solar tunnel is a cheaper alternative to a glass greenhouse. It is available in different sizes.

If you have limited space, it may be possible to house a lean-to greenhouse. Paint the wall inside the greenhouse white to give your plants extra light. A greenhouse designed to fit into a corner should be considered only if this is your only possible site.

Greenhouses are usually delivered in kit form for you to erect. A second pair of hands is very useful when putting up a greenhouse! Many suppliers will put up the greenhouse, if you would rather not be bothered with this job. There is obviously a charge for this service.

Siting

Ideally, a greenhouse should:

- stand on a level site;
- have its longer side facing south;
- be in full sun;
- have shelter from the prevailing wind;
- have easy access from the house;
- be near to mains water, gas and electricity.

In practice, it is seldom possible to achieve all of these ideals. What is more important is that the greenhouse fits in with the design of your garden and 'looks right'.

Making it easier

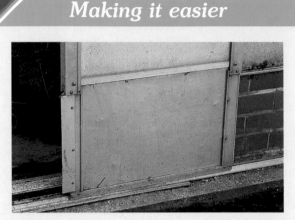

Many greenhouses are short of headroom. Some are only 165 cm (5 ft 6 in) at the highest point. You can overcome this by placing and securing the greenhouse on a low brick wall. This creates a problem, though – the door is not long enough. In this case, it is better to lengthen the door by fixing a panel to the bottom rather than lowering the sliding gear.

Ventilation

Ventilation is extremely important for both temperature and disease control. Few greenhouses are supplied with sufficient ventilation. One of the best ways of getting enough ventilation is to purchase a greenhouse with a sliding door at each end. The extra cost of having an additional door is money well spent. Where this is not possible, a louvre vent, fitted opposite the door and near to the floor, is more effective than additional roof vents. Unexpected sunshine, when you are out, can cause a rapid rise in temperature. This is prevented by having automatic vent openers; they are well worth the cost.

Greenhouses are often shaded to prevent over-heating and sun scorch. Well-ventilated greenhouses need the minimum of shading and possibly none at all. Your plants need light to grow, and shading should be confined to the south- and west-facing sides.

During very cold weather, plants sandwiched between polystyrene and fleece are well protected.

One of two automatic vent openers that lift a section of the roof in a Keder greenhouse.

Lighting

Even when the temperature is high enough, plants will not grow rapidly during dark winter days. Special lamps for supplementary lighting are available. These will increase plant growth but they are very inefficient because plants use less than 3% of available light.

Inside fittings

Staging

If you are to make full use of your greenhouse, you will need some form of staging. Slatted staging allows good air flow, which helps to control fungus disease, but it is cold in winter. A good compromise is to have slatted wood or galvanised 'weldmesh' staging for the summer, covering it in winter with polystyrene slabs protected by a plastic sheet. Cavity wall insulating slabs from a builders' merchant are ideal for this purpose.

Shelving

Narrow shelves above the staging give an additional area for pots and trays. Shelves are particularly useful for young plants that require a lot of light – tomatoes, for example. Don't fit wide shelves because they block too much light from the plants below them. Place trays under pots on top shelves to prevent drips on plants below.

Electricity

An electric light and electric socket, fitted by a qualified electrician, are extremely useful. They allow you to use an electric propagator in which seeds will germinate quickly and cuttings are more likely to succeed. An electric propagator can also be used to protect delicate plants during their first few weeks of growth.

The vents in the lid of many propagators are not effective because there is no air intake. A matchstick or garden label under the lid allows air flow and helps to clear condensation.

Heating and insulation

Maintaining growing temperatures in a small greenhouse is very expensive and seldom cost effective. Whatever the temperature, there will be very little plant growth in winter, because light levels are low. A heated greenhouse is necessary only if you are an enthusiast with a specialist plant collection.

However, keeping your greenhouse frost-free is very worthwhile and requires some form of heating. A heater with a thermostat set at around 5°C (41°F) will keep your greenhouse free from frost, provided it has a large enough output. A heater with large output does not necessarily use more fuel than one with a smaller output, as it will be burning for less time.

Paraffin, propane, natural gas and electricity are the common fuels for greenhouse heating. A paraffin heater is useful if you want a frost-free period for just a few weeks in spring. The disadvantages are that it needs daily attention, has a low heat output and has no thermostat. You should consider other heating methods if your greenhouse is to be kept frost-free all winter.

Propane gas (red cylinders) is suitable for greenhouse heaters; do not use butane (blue cylinders), because it may freeze on very cold nights. Gas heaters are fitted with various safety devices; for additional safety, keep the gas bottles outside the greenhouse and away from the house wall.

It is essential to have two cylinders and a change-over valve, as it is almost inevitable that the cylinder will run out during a time of peak use – on a frosty night. Note the polystyrene insulation inside the glass.

Where possible, consider using natural gas. It is completely trouble-free, very reliable and much cheaper than bottled gas. Most gas-fired greenhouse heaters can be adjusted to take either natural gas or propane.

Electricity is versatile and convenient. It is more expensive than natural gas but no more than the other options if you use 'Economy-7' or similar tariff. A fan heater fitted with an electronic thermostat is very cost effective and is particularly useful as it helps to prevent pockets of cold air. With the exception of electricity, all heaters produce water vapour, which increases condensation. They also produce carbon dioxide, which is essential for plant growth but is of no value here because low light limits plant growth when the heaters are on.

Reducing the running costs

All heated greenhouses should be insulated. The best insulation for the lower half is polystyrene slabs. Builders' merchants supply polystyrene slabs for cavity wall insulation, which happen to be the same width as standard greenhouse glass. The sheets last indefinitely, are economical and easy to fit. The upper part of the greenhouse can be lined with bubble plastic. Twin-wall plastic with large bubbles (5 cm; 2 in) is best. Take care not to buy packing material – a single sheet of plastic covered with small bubbles – because this is less effective. The glazing bars of most greenhouses have a channel on the inside; clips that lock into this channel and hold the bubble plastic in place are available from garden centres. In some types of greenhouses there is no channel at the corners. If yours is this type, secure the plastic by tying thin wire (or nylon string) to the construction bolts and adding an additional nut. When you remove the insulation, be sure to label each piece ready for refitting in the autumn.

Heat can be conserved by eliminating draughts, especially around the base and eaves of the greenhouse. Gas and paraffin heaters require air, so be careful that you do not seal the whole house. You can reduce heating costs by dividing the greenhouse into two sections: hang sheets of bubble plastic vertically across the width of the house and secure them at the sides to form a partition. You can then heat one section and treat the other as a cold greenhouse.

Below is given the heat output (measured in kilo-watts – kW) needed to keep a greenhouse frost-free.

Size of greenhouse	Recommended heat output (kW)
6 × 8 feet (approx 2 × 2.5 m)	1
8 × 10 feet (approx 2.5 × 3 m)	2
10 × 15 feet (approx 3 × 5 m)	4

Uses of greenhouses

Many greenhouses are a hive of activity during the spring and summer but are often unused for the rest of the year. Even a cold greenhouse can be used all the year round. Below are some suggestions for year-round use of a frost-free greenhouse; those that are also suitable for a cold greenhouse are marked *.

Year-round uses of a frost-free greenhouse

Winter (January)	Spring (April)	Summer (July)	Autumn (October)
Strawberries in pots or growing-bags*	Strawberries (in flower)*	Tomatoes, melons, cucumbers, aubergines*	Rooted cuttings of hardy perennials*
Sweet pea plants in Rootrainers*	Various brassicas and other vegetable and salad plants*	Pot plants and herbs from seed*	Bulbs for Christmas flowering*
Polyanthus (sown July)*	Chrysanthemum, fuchsia and dahlia cuttings	Seedlings of biennials (eg foxgloves)*	Chrysanthemums in flower for cutting*
Broad bean plants in Rootrainers*	Trays of bedding plants	Seedlings of perennials (eg aquilegia)*	Polyanthus and pansies from seed*
Half-hardy perennials from cuttings taken in the autumn	Seedlings of faster growing bedding plants	Softwood cuttings of shrubs*	Spring bulbs in pots for early flowering*
Geranium seedlings sown October	Hanging basket plants from seeds and cuttings		Containers of spring bulbs for patio*
Spring bulbs in pots planted in autumn*	Half-hardy indoor crop plants (eg tomatoes)		Rooted cuttings of half-hardy perennials
Parsley (cropping)*	Half-hardy outdoor crop plants (eg courgettes)		
Germinating seeds of: lobelia begonias onions parsley 'Hispi' cabbage			
Chrysanthemum stools in pots*			
Half-hardy shrubs in patio pots (eg fuchsia)			
Pots of half-hardy perennials (eg canna)			

A very useful propagator can be made with a soil-warming cable.

Making a propagator with a soil-warming cable

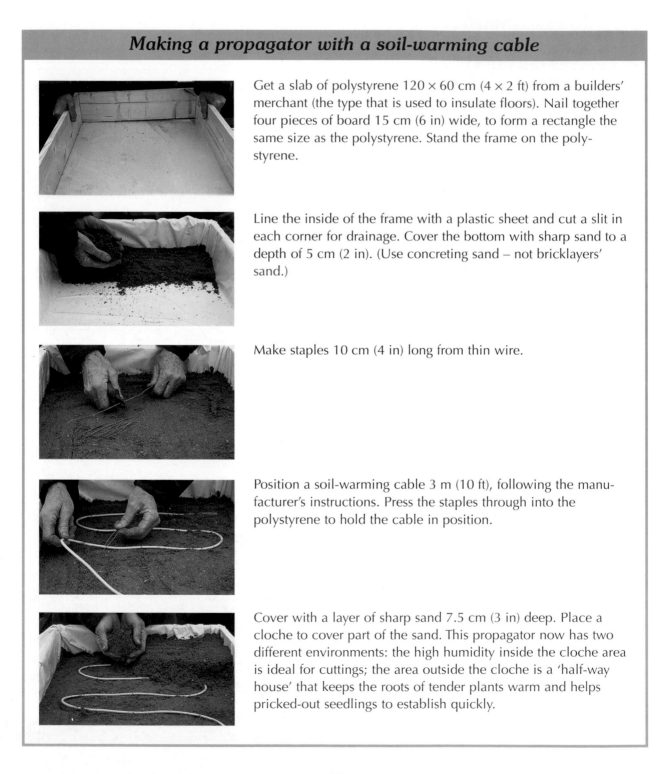

Get a slab of polystyrene 120 × 60 cm (4 × 2 ft) from a builders' merchant (the type that is used to insulate floors). Nail together four pieces of board 15 cm (6 in) wide, to form a rectangle the same size as the polystyrene. Stand the frame on the polystyrene.

Line the inside of the frame with a plastic sheet and cut a slit in each corner for drainage. Cover the bottom with sharp sand to a depth of 5 cm (2 in). (Use concreting sand – not bricklayers' sand.)

Make staples 10 cm (4 in) long from thin wire.

Position a soil-warming cable 3 m (10 ft), following the manufacturer's instructions. Press the staples through into the polystyrene to hold the cable in position.

Cover with a layer of sharp sand 7.5 cm (3 in) deep. Place a cloche to cover part of the sand. This propagator now has two different environments: the high humidity inside the cloche area is ideal for cuttings; the area outside the cloche is a 'half-way house' that keeps the roots of tender plants warm and helps pricked-out seedlings to establish quickly.

Seedlings can be started off in your house and transferred to the greenhouse for growing on. Various windowsill propagators are available for this purpose. Propagators that supply a little bottom heat are more successful than those that don't – especially when you use them to root cuttings.

An electric propagator designed to go on a windowsill. Separate trays make it very versatile. The three centre trays are the warmest and should be used for seeds such as begonias and lobelia. Raise the lid slightly with a matchstick to admit air and make the ventilators more effective.

Using windowsill propagators

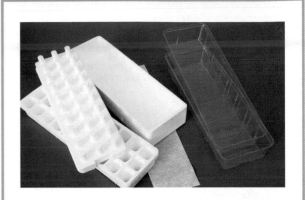

This windowsill propagator includes a reservoir that keeps the plants moist for up to three weeks. Each cell has a square top and large round hole at the bottom. This shape prevents the compost from falling out.

1 Fill the cells with compost and firm it gently with the legs of the inner section. Add more compost if necessary.

2 Put the inner section, complete with the capillary matting, into the water container. (Capillary matting soaks water from the reservoir to the base of the plant cells.) Make sure that the end of the matting reaches all the way to the bottom of the water.

3 Place the tray of compost-filled cells onto the matting and prick out one seedling, or sow one seed, into each cell. Position the tray on a north- or east-facing windowsill and cover it with the plastic hood. If you place a foil-covered card between the room and the propagator, this will reflect light back onto the plants.

4 Arrange kitchen foil to reflect light onto the room side of the plants.

5 When the plants are ready for potting up, use the legs on the inner section to push them from the cells.

Growing mediums

Even the best soil is unsuitable for filling plant pots and trays, because it does not hold sufficient air or water. The material used for pots and trays is called compost – not to be confused with the compost of the compost bin. To avoid confusion, compost from the bin is called 'garden compost' throughout this book.

Most composts available do not contain any soil. They are light, easy to use and give excellent results. John Innes composts contain a large proportion of soil and are much heavier. Soil-less composts are suitable for all pots, baskets and containers of annuals. Always use a soil-based compost for long-term planting of shrubs and trees in containers.

Many soil-less composts are made from peat with added nutrients and a wetting agent. This is a pity, because our peat bogs have taken thousands of years to form and are now rapidly disappearing. There are several good peat-free composts that are made from bark, chipboard waste, coir and various other waste materials. It is false economy to buy cheap compost; your first choice should always be a good quality peat alternative. Acid composts (ericaceous) are necessary for plants that require acid soils (eg heathers and azaleas). Multipurpose compost is suitable for most greenhouse purposes. Use multipurpose compost for sowing, hanging baskets, potting up and filling containers. This is more convenient than having a separate compost for sowing seeds.

> **Note** The material in a growing-bag may be suitable for growing tomatoes but it is an inferior product and you should not use it as a compost substitute.

Growing-bags

Growing-bags are an easy and convenient way to grow crop plants but you must pay careful attention to watering and feeding. Staking plants in growing-bags can present some difficulty – take care not to pierce the bottom of the bag. If you intend using growing-bags, buy the very best quality available. Cheap ones contain inferior material and will produce poor quality results.

Sowing seeds

Seed trays are usually too large for sowing seeds; a plant pot is more suitable. Square plant pots are useful for seeds, as they pack neatly into a propagator.

Loosely fill a plant pot to the brim with multi-purpose compost. Tap the pot gently on the

bench to consolidate the compost, and add more if necessary; then water it using a fine 'rose' on the watering can.

Sprinkle the seeds thinly over the surface, as evenly as possible.

Cover the seeds with vermiculite. (Vermiculite is more suitable here than compost because it allows light to get to the seeds. It weighs almost nothing and the smallest shoot can push through.) Insert a label, with seed type and sowing date written on it, between the pot edge and the compost and place in a propagator. The propagator should be in good light but not in direct sunlight.

One pot is sown thinly, the other normally and the third is thickly sown. Note that in all three pots the seeds are sown evenly.

Note The first two leaves (seed leaves) that appear on a seedling have a different shape from later leaves (true leaves). Some plants (eg grass) have only one seed leaf.

Pricking out

Transplanting seedlings to give each one space to develop is known as 'pricking out'. The best time to prick out is when the seed leaves are fully expanded and before the true leaves begin to appear. Seedlings can be pricked out into trays, cells or pots. Fill the container with multipurpose compost, and water through a fine rose.

Use a small dibber, garden label or similar to ease the seedlings upwards. Holding a single seedling by its leaf (*never* by the stem), lift it clear of the pot.

Make a hole with the dibber and lower the seedling into it. If the root is very long, spiral it into the hole. Bury all but a small portion of the stem; the leaves should be just clear of the compost.

Gently press a little compost around the stem to fill the hole and keep the seedling in position. When the tray is full, place it in good light but not direct sunlight.

Growing in plant pots

The base of a plastic plant pot is well supplied with holes and, for most purposes, additional drainage material is not required.

Potting up

The process of transplanting a single plant into a plant pot is known as 'potting up'.

Potting on

'Potting on' is the transfer of a plant from one pot to a larger one. It is possible to pot up a small plant directly into a large pot but very much better root systems are formed if you pot on a number of times to increasingly larger pots. This also makes much better use of greenhouse space.

Potting on

The new plant pot needs to be one or two (no more) sizes larger than the old one. Put multipurpose compost in the bottom. Place the plant on the compost, add or remove compost until the surface of the old compost round the plant is slightly below the top of the larger pot.

Note When you pot on tomatoes and cucumbers, place the plant in the pot before adding any compost. The buried stem will produce additional roots and increase the vigour of the plant.   *cont'd*

Carefully tap the edge of the old pot on the bench to free the plant. Lift off the pot. If roots are coiling around the bottom of the pot, tease them out gently.

Position the plant in the centre of the pot and fill the space with multipurpose compost.

Firm the compost with your thumbs and add more as necessary. Your thumbs should be in contact with the inner edge of the pot throughout this operation, as pressure near to the stem might damage the roots.

in the east and west, so windows facing those directions are okay. A cool room is better than a hot one but the windowsill must be frost-free. Make sure that your plants are on the room side of the curtains if they are drawn at night.

A good multipurpose compost will contain sufficient nutrients for your plants' needs but add a little seaweed extract to the water once a week.

Growing plug plants

Do not attempt to pull the plants from the modules. Use a short piece of thin cane to push them from the bottom.

Insert each plug into the centre of a pot of multipurpose compost.

Gently firm the compost around the plug.

Transferring plug plants to individual 7.5 cm (3 in) pots takes a lot of compost, time and space.

Plug plants

Plug plants offer a short cut to success. They are available in garden centres and by mail order. Some plug plants are sold as 'garden ready' but in practice all plug plants (including vegetables) need to 'grow on' before being planted outside. Remove plug plants from their 'modules' as soon as possible.

A greenhouse is the ideal place to grow plug plants until they are large enough for planting in the garden. If you do not have the luxury of a greenhouse, there are ways that you can make a windowsill more plant-friendly. Avoid a south-facing window, because direct sun may be harmful. In early spring and late autumn the sun is low when

Empty modules

The best thing to do with empty modules is throw them away. Trying to grow your own plug plants is rather a waste of time. Sowing seeds in a pot and pricking out into small pots or Rootrainers will be more successful.

Making it easier

Using Rootrainers

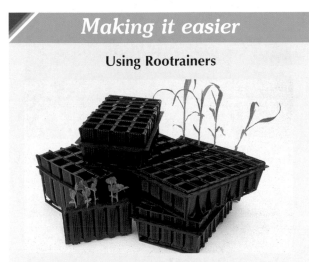

There are four different sizes of Rootrainers.

Rootrainers were developed in Canada for growing trees. They are also an ideal way to raise garden plants. Each plant is held in an individual cell, designed to develop a good root system. The cells open to release the plants without disturbing the roots. The best way to grow on plug plants is to transfer them to the Rootrainer named 'Shrub', which is 7.5 cm (3 in) deep. A tray holds 32 cells. Each plant then develops its own excellent root system that can be transplanted without disturbance. Rootrainers are reusable and, with care, will last for many years.

The other sizes of Rootrainers are used for larger plants. 'Fleet' is the largest size, with cells that are 18 cm (7 in) deep and are ideal for sweet peas, beans, sweetcorn and the brassicas. 'Fleet' holders carry 40 cells. 'Rannoch' has narrow cells 10 cm (4 in) deep, which you can use for plants such as lobelia, ideal for hanging baskets. There are 50 cells per tray.

'Sherwood' is a general-purpose Rootrainer; there are 32 cells 12.5 cm (5 in) deep per tray. Trays that hold 24 cells of 'Sherwood' or 'Shrub' are also available.

Take a Rootrainer and fill it with moist multi-purpose compost. Water with a rose can. Make a small hole in the top of a single cell and insert a plug plant.

Stand the Rootrainers on two upright plant pots. When the roots emerge from the bottom of the cells, they dry up and the root tip dies. This encourages many side roots to form higher in the cell.

In a very short time the roots of the plug plant will have filled the Rootrainer cell, and the plants are ready for hardening off (see p 26).

Watering

A haws-type watering can with a rose park. A 'haws' can is this general shape and has a fitting (a 'rose park') to hold the rose when it is not needed. Its long reach makes it ideal for use in the greenhouse.

Watering plants is quite a skill – too little and they die, too much and they die. You are more likely to kill a plant by over-watering than under-watering. You can easily spot a plant that is short of water – the foliage goes dull and it begins to wilt. Moreover, the pot feels very light when you lift it. A plant in the first stages of wilting soon recovers after being watered. A plant with too much water also wilts but, by the time it does, it is almost too late to do much about it. If you notice a wilting plant, feel its weight before adding water – it might be too wet rather than too dry.

An attempt to save an over-watered plant. Remove the pot and stand the plant on several layers of newspaper. Next day replace the plant in the pot.

Making it easier

An electronic water meter. This device registers the amount of water in the soil or compost. It is very useful for house and container plants that are too heavy to lift.

Growing from cuttings

Growing from cuttings is an easy and cheap way for you to obtain more plants. It is also an excellent way to keep your half-hardy perennials from year to year. In late summer, take a few cuttings from container plants, hanging basket plants and half-hardy border plants. Root them in the greenhouse and pot them up. These will survive the winter in a frost-free greenhouse, provided you do not allow them to become too wet or too dry. In early spring, bring them into growth by feeding and watering. During March and April use their new growth for another lot of cuttings. One plant will produce many cuttings and you will have lots of plants for baskets, containers and borders. When you have enough rooted cuttings, discard the stock plants (plants kept to produce cuttings).

The way to take cuttings is similar for most plants. Select young shoots without flower buds wherever possible. If all shoots contain flower buds, pinch them out as you prepare the cutting.

Collecting cuttings in a plastic bag helps to stop them from drying out.

Growing from cuttings

Prepare each cutting by making a clean cut under a leaf joint and stripping the leaves and buds from the lower half of the stem. If the remaining leaf area is rather large, cut away half of the two lower leaves.

Dip the cut end in a little rooting powder. This speeds up rooting and prevents fungus disease.

Cuttings root easily in Jiffy7s, which are compressed pellets of peat and coir held in a biodegradable net. They expand to full size when soaked in water for ten minutes. Fill the bottom third of a tray with multipurpose compost and pack the Jiffy7s on top.

Insert one cutting into each Jiffy7 and place the tray in a heated propagator. The propagator needs to be in good light but not in direct sunlight.

When the roots appear through the side of the Jiffy7, pot up into a small pot. There is no need to remove the net, as it will rot away.

Cuttings can also be rooted in rockwool blocks and various mixtures of sharp sand with compost. A mixture of half perlite and half compost is also quite successful. In fact, any mix that gives the base of the cutting a supply of air and water will encourage rooting. Temperature is also important: cuttings root much more readily with a little bottom heat.

Hardening off

Preparing a greenhouse plant to withstand outside conditions is called 'hardening off'. Greenhouse plants are more tender and have softer tissues than similar ones growing outside. A plant taken direct from the greenhouse to the garden will not flourish outside, and may even die. Greenhouse plants will thrive outside if you give them a gradual change of environment. The time taken to harden a plant off depends on the time of year and the weather. In spring, hardening off may take as long as three weeks but may be unnecessary during the height of summer.

There are four main ways of hardening off:

- Transfer plants from your greenhouse to a cold frame and, after a week, give increasing ventilation until the frame is open day and night.

- Put the plants outside in the daytime and inside at night. After ten days or so the plants can be left outside on still, mild nights.

- Place the plants outside and cover them with two layers of fleece. Remove one layer in the daytime and, a week later, remove both layers during the day, replacing a single one at night.

- Plant out under ventilated cloches that have been in position for the previous two weeks. Increase the ventilation during the daytime and, after a week or so, remove the cloches during the day and replace them at night. After another week the cloches can be left off altogether.

Whichever method you use, the timing must be adjusted according to the weather. Never allow plants being hardened off to get frosted or be subjected to drying winds. It is important to continue watering and feeding during the hardening off period.

> *Note* Greenhouse seedlings that are stroked regularly develop stronger stems than those that are not. (Run your hand gently over the seedlings as you would stroke a cat.)

Table-top gardening

Link-a-Board being used for a table-top garden.

Table-top gardening in a greenhouse, a conservatory or on the patio can be very productive. A table-top garden can be tended from a standing position with no bending involved – provided you have someone to help lift the compost onto the table. With a low table, this type of gardening is also possible from a stool, chair or wheelchair. Carrots, lettuce, radish, turnips, beetroot, kohlrabi, some herbs and lots of different stir-fry leaves are easy to grow. Cover the table (or staging) with a sheet of plastic and position a surround round the edges – there is no need for a bottom. The surround needs to be around 15 cm (6 in) deep; it can be made from wood but plastic is better. Fill the table top with multipurpose compost, water and sow or plant. Use a very small watering can that is easy to lift and will wet the compost between the plants without knocking them over. You should be able to take several crops from one filling but you must feed with a liquid fertiliser. A small area can be very productive, especially if you select quick-maturing varieties. Your table-top garden need not be confined to food plants – you can experiment with a whole range of fast-growing annuals, including some trailing plants.

Food from the greenhouse

Your greenhouse can make a large contribution to home-grown food. There are many advantages in raising salad, herb and vegetable plants for outside planting, rather than sowing directly into the soil. In addition, plants from warmer climates can be grown successfully, tomatoes being the prime example.

Tomatoes

A good reason for growing your own tomatoes is that you can be certain that they are free from chemical spray residues. In addition, greenhouse tomatoes taste much better than any from the supermarkets. A greenhouse tomato, picked and eaten immediately, has a far superior flavour. One reason for this is freshness; another is that the fruit is warm. Tomatoes at refrigerator temperature are rather bland. A further reason for better flavour is that supermarket tomatoes have to withstand travel; many of the best-flavoured varieties do not travel well.

Which variety?

With over 3,000 tomato varieties to select from, your greenhouse should never house only one. Growing several different varieties adds interest and is an insurance against choosing an inferior one. Possibly the best variety for flavour, yield, earliness and ease of growing is 'Gardener's Delight'. The fruits are red, smaller than standard varieties but larger than cherry varieties. One of the best cherry varieties is 'Sweet 100'. Other good varieties include: 'Sunbelle' – small and yellow; 'Shirley' – red, normal size and disease resistant; 'Big Boy' – a large, red, beefsteak tomato with few seeds and best for cooking. The beefsteak variety 'Brandy Wine' has an outstanding flavour.

Raising tomato plants

It is not easy to buy good tomato plants. Many on offer are weak stemmed and spindly. Plants that have been on display for some time may be affected by too much heat and not enough light. Plants bought at the roadside may carry whitefly or other problems. In all outlets the choice of variety is limited. If you have a propagator and a frost-free greenhouse, raising your own from seed is the best method.

Growing tomato plants from seed

- Use top-quality peat-free compost.
- Sow in late February for an early crop.
- Sow the main crop four weeks later.
- Germinate in a heated propagator.
- Prick out as soon as the seed leaves are fully expanded.
- Prick out into individual 7.5 cm (3 in) pots of multipurpose compost.
- Place the pots in the propagator.
- When the plants are too tall for the propagator, move them to the greenhouse staging.
- On cold nights, cover them with one or two layers of fleece.
- Do not let the plants touch; move them further apart as they grow.
- Feed once a week with a weak solution of a liquid feed.
- Add a little seaweed extract to the feed.
- Pot on to 12.5 cm (5 in) pots when the roots appear in the drainage holes.
- Stake each plant with a split cane and tie loosely with soft string.
- Pot on into 22.5 cm (9 in) pots or in their fruiting positions.

Training

Grow your tomatoes as tall, single stem plants (cordons). This makes the best use of your greenhouse, because cordons will fill otherwise empty roof space. Train your tomato plants by removing the side shoots ('pinching out') when they are less than 5 cm (2 in) long. One side shoot (sometimes two) will appear at the base of each leaf.

Bush varieties have a different growth habit and cannot be trained as cordons. These need to be in patio containers or on your vegetable plot, as they have a spreading habit and take a lot of horizontal space.

Support

Your cordon tomatoes will need supporting. One good method is to attach a string to the greenhouse glazing bar above each plant and tie the other end loosely around the stem towards the bottom of the plant. As the plant grows, twist the top round the string.

Pollination

Tomatoes are self-fertile. In order for the fruit to 'set', pollen must move from the anthers (male parts of the flowers) to the stigmas (female parts). When the first flowers open, give each plant a daily shake to get the pollen moving.

Feeding

When the first tomatoes have 'set' (ie they are the size of peas), regular feeding is essential. Use a fertiliser formulated for tomatoes, as it will have the correct balance of nutrients. Several specialist feeds are available, including an organic one. Follow the instructions on the container and add a little seaweed extract to the solution before you apply it. The instructions will tell you how much feed to add to the watering can but few say how much of the resulting solution each plant needs. Keep an eye on the new growth at the top of the plant: if it is green and vigorous, you are giving enough; if the top is pale and weak, increase the amount or the frequency of the feed.

Leaf removal

As the plants grow, the bottom leaves become shaded. They may curl and go yellow. Snap such leaves off with an upward movement: removing them improves the air flow around the plants. Never take more than one or two at a time, and leave all healthy leaves intact.

'Stopping'

After four or five trusses (bunches of tomatoes) have set, it is common practice to break the top off each plant. This is known as 'stopping'. If you live in a cold part of the country, stop your plants above the fifth truss, because your season is too short to ripen more. In warmer areas, stopping is unnecessary; most plants will produce at least a dozen trusses. When plants reach the greenhouse roof, it may be possible to train them horizontally. Another method is to lower the plants by releasing the ties and laying the bare portion of the stems on the floor. Retie the string to support the top of the plant with the leaves, fruit and flowers in a vertical position.

Ripening

Tomatoes in a cold greenhouse are sometimes slow to begin ripening. Placing an over-ripe banana on a bottom truss will trigger the ripening process.

Growing methods

The most popular way to grow tomatoes is in growing-bags – three plants to a bag. This method can work well, provided that you use top-quality bags. Never be tempted to buy cheap growing-bags. Growing two plants per bag will probably give a higher yield than the usual three.

Tip

When you plant tomatoes into their final position, push a single clove of garlic into the soil or compost 7.5 cm (3 in) away from the stem with the tip left showing. The garlic will grow but fail to develop. The tomato will have a better flavour and be less likely to suffer insect damage.

Making it easier

GroPots with a crop of 'Gardener's Delight' tomatoes.

Growing-bags are not very easy to water. The various methods of funnels, drips, soaker hoses and so on are either very fiddly or not very satisfactory. I find that the easiest method is to use GroPots. Plant the tomatoes as deeply as possible and fill the inner ring with additional compost.

The Bulrush System

A system has been developed that allows tomatoes to be left untended for a week or more.

1 Place the inner liner inside the large box and position the lid.

2 Cut three holes in the base of the growing-bag to correspond with the holes in the lid.

3 Cut out the planting holes, put your hand into each hole and work compost into the tube beneath. Plant a tomato in each hole.

4 Fill the base with the nutrient solution provided. There is sufficient water to last for well over a week – the actual time depends upon the size of the plants.

This system works well and keeps the plants in production longer than other methods. You should water the compost in the growing-bag as well as keeping the base topped up. If you are going to leave your greenhouse untended for a week, grow plants with small fruits because beefsteak varieties are more subject to blossom end rot (see p 133).

Cucumbers

The cucumber plant is a climber and needs supports at least 1.5 m (5 ft) high and wide. A net with 10 cm (4 in) squares on a wooden frame is ideal. A single plant usually produces more fruits than one household can use. The plant will often collapse after it has produced its first flush of fruits. You can insure against this by sowing one or two seeds every four weeks from March to June.

The cucumber has single-sex flowers and, unlike other plants, its fruits form from unpollinated as well as pollinated flowers. The fruits from pollinated flowers are bitter, so remove all male flowers before they open. This is not easy: the plant grows very fast and produces male flowers in almost every node.

Note The stalk of a female flower consists of a tiny cucumber, whereas the stalk of a male flower is a plain stem.

Select a cucumber variety that has only female flowers. Then you won't have to search for and remove male flowers!

The all-female variety Petita produces cucumbers that are an ideal size for a small family. If you want larger cucumbers, Pepinex is a good variety for the home gardener.

Try this. A cucumber plant benefits from rooting into two growing-bags placed one over the other. Large connecting holes were cut in the top of the bottom bag and the bottom of the top bag.

Growing cucumbers

- One-third fill a clean 15 cm (6 in) pot with moist multipurpose compost.
- Push one seed edgeways, half way into the compost.
- Place the pot in a heated propagator on a high setting.
- As the seedling grows, add more compost until the pot is full.
- Keep the plant well watered but do not allow a pool to form at the base of the stem.
- Feed once a week with half-strength tomato fertiliser.
- When the roots fill the pot and before they begin to circle, pot on to a 30 cm (12 in) pot, or a growing-bag, positioned by the supports.
- Tie the main stem vertically in the centre of the supports. Remove all side shoots and flowers from the bottom 20 cm (8 in) of the main stem, to keep the crop off the floor.
- As new side shoots appear, tie them horizontally on the supports until the frame is covered.
- Remove all other side shoots as they appear, including side shoots on side shoots.
- Water regularly and do not allow the compost to become dry. Damp down (ie wet the floor) after watering to maintain a humid atmosphere.
- Continue to feed once a week with half-strength tomato fertiliser.
- Harvest the cucumbers as soon as the lower ends are becoming rounded.
- Use secateurs or a knife to harvest; regular harvesting increases the yield.
- When the first fruits have been harvested, fix a plastic ring (eg the central section of a large squash bottle) round the base of the stem, secure it with string and fill with compost. The stem will grow additional roots and the plant will have renewed vigour.

31

Melons

Melons are grown in a similar way to cucumbers except that the female flowers (ie the flowers with a tiny melon on the stalk) must be pollinated by introducing pollen from a male flower on a little cotton wool. When the melon begins to swell, pinch off the shoot one leaf beyond. 'Sweetheart' is a reliable variety.

Peppers

Peppers grow well in an unheated greenhouse and give a very worthwhile crop. Unlike tomatoes and cucumbers, they freeze well so a temporary glut will not be a problem. Green peppers ripen into red or some other colour if they are left on the plant. Ripening is very slow, and you will get a larger crop if you harvest only green fruit.

Growing peppers

- Sow seeds in March and germinate in a propagator.
- Prick out seedlings into 10 cm (4 in) pots of multipurpose compost and place on staging.
- If frost is forecast, cover the plants with fleece at night.
- Pot on into 22.5 cm (9 in) pots of multi-purpose compost or into growing-bags – three plants per bag.
- Support each plant with a single cane and string tie.
- Water regularly and feed each week with tomato fertiliser and seaweed extract.
- Harvest the fruit as soon as they are a reasonable size; cut through the stalk with a sharp knife.

Aubergines

Aubergines are grown in exactly the same way as peppers. Harvest the fruits while they are still shiny.

A board is placed under this aubergine to protect it from the soil.

Early strawberries

Strawberries grown in a cold greenhouse can be harvested four weeks or more before the crop grown outside. The plants should be propagated from an outside crop during July or August.

Growing strawberries from seed

Strawberries can be grown from seed. Sow the variety 'Temptation' in January, pot on to 22.5 cm (9 in) pots, and you will be picking strawberries from July to October.

Propagating strawberries from runners

Thread a length of string through two of the holes in the bottom of a 12.5 cm (5 in) plant pot and fill it with multipurpose compost.

Place the runner over the compost and tie the strings to hold it in position.

Keep the compost moist and a few weeks later you will have a well-rooted plant. Cut the string and transplant into a strawberry tub, an old growing-bag or a larger pot. Leave the plant outside to get frosted, as this helps bud formation. In January transfer the plant to a cold greenhouse or cold frame. Give a feed in March; when the flowers open, dust them with a little cotton wool to assist pollination. After the harvest is complete, throw the plants away, as they will not force successfully a second year.

Salads and herbs

Salads and herbs can be grown in pots throughout the growing season. Loose leaf lettuce performs better in a pot than the hearted types. Do not attempt to grow summer lettuce in winter; choose a winter variety such as Kellys but be prepared for some very slow growth.

Flowers from the greenhouse

In addition to providing quality food, a greenhouse can supply almost continuous colour to your home and your garden. Bedding plants, basket plants, container plants, half-hardy border perennials, hardy border perennials, biennials, pot plants and cut flowers are all easy and rewarding to grow.

Chrysanthemums

Chrysanthemums fit in very well with tomatoes. Pot-grown chrysanthemums stand outside during the summer and are brought in for flowering in early October when the tomatoes are coming to an end.

Cress in pots is ready for harvest in a little more than a week. This has a better flavour than the punnets on offer in the supermarkets.

Chrysanthemum plants that were supplied by post six months earlier.

The ideal way to start growing chrysanthemums is to buy rooted cuttings of October/November flowering plants in May. Buy from a specialist nursery, as their plants will be disease-free. Chrysanthemums are fairly hardy but the cuttings need protection from frost.

Growing chrysanthemums

- Pot up the rooted cuttings individually in 9 cm (3.5 in) pots of multipurpose compost and grow on the greenhouse staging.
- Pinch off the top, leaving four or five leaves below; this causes four or five stems to grow instead of only one.
- Two weeks later, pot on to 22.5 cm (9 in) pots and harden off.
- Insert a garden cane and tie with string to support the stems.
- Stand the pots outside throughout the summer.
- Attach the tops of the canes to a horizontal wire fixed to two strong supports, to prevent them from blowing over.
- Water as needed and feed weekly with tomato fertiliser.
- In the autumn, use fleece to protect the buds from frost.
- In early October, transfer the pots to the greenhouse for flowering.
- Cut the flowers when the outside petals are expanded and the centre petals are still tightly packed.
- Crush the end of the flower stem and place in water.

Disbudding

'Disbudding' is the removal of flower buds to control the size and number of flowers and the length of flowerless stem. Chrysanthemum varieties are either sprays (several flowers on a single stem) or blooms (a single large flower on a stem). Disbudding methods are different for the two types.

Spray chrysanthemums

If the top bud is much larger than the nearest buds, pinch it out. Leave the top eight or nine buds and remove the lower ones to give a length of clear stem.

Blooms

Remove all the buds and side shoots below the top bud. Disbud when the buds are large enough to handle.

After flowering, cut off any growth above 15 cm (6 in) and place the pots under the staging. During the winter, give only sufficient water to prevent the plant from drying out. In March put the pots in better light and increase watering enough to keep the compost moist. Take cuttings from the new growth and discard the stool (the roots and ground level parts of the plant).

When disbudded, this plant had the lower buds left intact. This resulted in a second crop of smaller flowers.

Note Your stock will gradually deteriorate. To overcome this, buy new plants every third or fourth year.

Bulbs

Spring bulbs flower about one month early in a cold greenhouse. Plant up bulbs in the autumn in 22.5 cm (9 in) pots and water throughout the winter, giving just enough to prevent the compost from drying out. Frost will not harm the foliage but do not allow the pots to become frozen. (One way to prevent this is to plunge them in a soil bed.) Cut the blooms as the flowers are about to open.

In addition to the usual daffodils and tulips, try a few less well known ones such as ranunculus.

Note To prevent tulip heads from hanging, prick the stem with a fine needle several times just below the flower.

Bowls of hyacinths

Bowl of hyacinths produced by the method described below.

Prepared hyacinths (for Christmas flowering) planted in a bowl often disappoint, because the bulbs do not flower at the same time. This is easily prevented. Plant a dozen or more prepared hyacinths in separate 7.5 cm (3 in) pots of multipurpose compost. Grow on the staging until the flower buds become visible between the leaves. Sort the bulbs into groups according to how advanced they are. Transfer the most advanced group to bowls of threes, fours or fives and move them into the house. These bulbs will all flower at the same time. Leave the less advanced groups to develop before treating them in the same way.

Grasses

Fuchsias

Grass flowers ready for cutting and drying.

Spare room on the staging during the summer can be used to grow ornamental grasses. Sow a few seeds in 12.5 cm (5 in) pots. Several of the annual ornamental grasses will flower in as little as ten weeks after sowing.

Fuchsia cuttings root easily and grow quickly. Grow your own standard fuchsias by removing all the side shoots. Pot on in the usual way. When the plant is at the required height, leave the top side shoots intact. A March cutting can become a standard 90 cm (3 ft) high by June.

Pot plants

A greenhouse can be a useful source of pot plants for the house.

Foliage plants from seed

Trees can make useful foliage plants but be prepared to throw them away if they become too large or lose their shape. Sow a large seed from an avocado pear in a 12.5 cm (5 in) pot and germinate in a propagator. The resulting plant will remain attractive for two years or so before you have to discard it. Several of the eucalyptus species make attractive pot plants; my favourite is 'Citriodora' because the leaves have an attractive perfume. Other trees from seed include grevillea and jacaranda. Sow unroasted coffee beans for a coffee plant.

Asparagus fern grows well from seed but makes little growth during the first year. Later the growth is rapid and the plants, which need little attention, make good pot plants. One or two pots, kept under the staging, yield lots of foliage useful for flower arrangements.

The foliage plant coleus is easy to grow from seed. Sow the seeds very thinly and do not prick them out until the first true leaves appear. In this way you can select the prettiest leaves and discard the others. Pot them up individually and pinch out the top to create a bushy plant. Pinch off the flower buds regularly or it will become straggly. If you get a colour you particularly like, propagate it from stem cuttings (see p 25); the new plants will have exactly the same colouring.

Flowering plants

Scizanthus in a 12.5 cm (5 in) pot – the seed was sown 12 weeks earlier.

A few stocks flowering in the greenhouse give it a lovely smell. Sow Brompton stocks in July, and grow on in pots. In October use them to replace the tomatoes. Water and feed in April for that scent; leave the single flowers to perfume the greenhouse and cut the double ones for displaying in the house. Unlike with most other stocks, it is not possible to tell if a seedling is a single or a double.

Note In milder parts of the country, Brompton stocks survive outside in sheltered gardens.

Chapter 3

Lawns and Trees

Decking, slabs, concrete or plastic membrane covered with gravel are all very well but there is nothing to beat the green carpet of a beautiful lawn. Green is the restful colour nature intended us to live with. A neatly cut and edged lawn gives real pleasure and is the perfect setting for beautiful beds and borders.

Lawns have other uses, too – play areas for the grandchildren or a place to sit, relax and enjoy the garden with its wildlife. When the sun does shine, the lawn is a place to erect a gazebo and enjoy a meal outside.

A lawn is a carpet of living plants that need as much care as the other garden plants. This means watering, weeding, feeding and cutting but no staking!

A new lawn

Turf

Laying turf can convert a bare patch of soil into a lawn in a single day. Turf is more expensive than seed and the quality is sometimes rather poor. Much of the turf on offer is cut from farmers' fields and may contain agricultural grasses that were bred for rapid growth. It is possible to buy good turf but at a price. Be sure to lay it correctly. Prepare the soil well in advance by digging or rotavating. If you rotavate, fork out all perennial weeds, and their underground parts, before starting. Level the area by raking it over a number of times, drawing soil from the higher parts to the hollows. Hold the rake handle fairly near to the ground and work the rake to and fro, pushing as well as pulling the soil. A sloping lawn still needs to be free from bumps and hollows. The soil should then be left to settle for several weeks before you lay the turf.

Making it easier

The easiest way to clear perennial weeds from an area intended for a lawn is to spray with glyphosate. This will be most effective if the weeds are actively growing and have plenty of leaves to absorb the spray.

A spade is not a very good tool for cutting turfs; use a lawn edging tool but make sure that it is sharp.

When the turfs arrive, scatter a layer 1 cm (0.5 in) deep of a mixture containing equal parts of peat substitute and sharp sand. Rake over for the last time, working backwards to remove all your foot marks. Do not tread on the soil after the final raking. Lay the first row of turf by the path, butting the edges together.

Where the turf is too large to fill the space:

- overlap the turfs;

- use the edge of the top turf as a guide;

- cut the lower turf with the edging tool;

- lift the top turf and remove the piece underneath;

- the top turf will now fit snugly in place.

Place a plank on the newly laid turf to stand on while you lay the next row. Walk only on planks laid across the new turf. Wait until the grass is growing before walking on the new lawn. Set the mower blades a little higher than normal for the first two cuts.

From seed

Growing a lawn from seed is a slower process – but you should finish up with a better lawn as well as one that fits your needs. If your lawn is for pure decoration, sow seeds of very fine grasses, such as fescues and bents. If your lawn is intended for heavy use, sow a mixture with a high proportion of rye grass. The best general-purpose lawns have a mixture of grasses – this gives a tough rye grass cover with the finer grasses forming a dense layer between and beneath. Soaking grass seed for 48 hours before sowing speeds up germination but wet seeds are more difficult to sow evenly. You can sow seed in April but September is the ideal time.

Care of an established lawn

Lawn care consisting of regular cutting and the odd treatment for broad-leaved weeds is insufficient. The cutting season produces a lot of grass and its removal impoverishes the soil. In order to get a

Ten steps to making a perfect lawn from seed

1 Dig over the area, removing any couch grass roots or any other perennial weeds. Apply 40 g per sq m (1 oz/sq yd) of growmore fertiliser or an organic substitute.

2 Leave the ground to settle for at least one week.

3 In spring wait until the soil has warmed to 10°C (50°F). In autumn make sure that the ground is not too dry for germination.

4 Rake the ground level, leaving a fine tilth on the surface. Keep the raking to a minimum, as too much may damage the soil structure.

5 Using string and pegs, divide the area into metre squares.

6 Mix the seed thoroughly and weigh it into 28 g (1 oz) lots. (Some seed mixtures may require a different amount; follow the instructions on the packet.)

7 Spread 28 g of seed evenly over each square.

8 Remove the strings and rake over very lightly, one section at a time – avoid walking on the sown area.

9 Water each section with a watering can fitted with a fine rose.

10 Cover with fleece, which you should remove soon after germination and before the grass grows through.

If the area is too large for a fleece cover to be practical, it should be watered in dry weather. Hang some old compact disks over the area or other shiny objects to keep the birds off (CDs often arrive by post or in magazines, and most are never used.) When the grass is growing away strongly, make the first cut. Set the mower blades fairly high and trim off the top 20 per cent of growth.

good lawn the soil must be fed. Mulching is not an option so some type of fertiliser is needed. Apply fertiliser in both spring and autumn. Spring fertiliser contains extra nitrogen and is unsuitable for the autumn feed. Be sure to apply fertiliser evenly; otherwise, the lawn becomes patchy. Apply only the recommended amount, as too much fertiliser is harmful and may burn the grass – scoop up any spillage and flood the area with water.

Do not apply fertiliser to a very dry lawn; give it a good watering first.

Weed control

A well cared for lawn will have few weeds, because the thick sward will prevent their growth. The odd weeds that do appear are best spot treated with a hormone weed-killer. If there are expanding patches of weeds in several different areas, it is better to treat the whole lawn. Hormone weed-killers are very effective when used according to the instructions. Your first cut after a treatment will contain weed-killer and must not be composted or used as a mulch.

Mowing

Regular mowing is essential. A regular cut takes less time and effort than infrequent heavy mowing when the grass has been allowed to get too high.

Fertiliser is not easy to apply evenly by hand. Light and dark patches often result and, worse still, the odd burnt patch. The wheeled spreader in the photograph has a very positive shut-off and gives an even spread – provided you can see the wheel marks to follow on the next pass.

This hand-held spreader is easy to use and takes very little time. Set it at a low rate and walk over the lawn in both directions, turning the handle as you go. Some fertiliser will spread on the edge of the borders; this is not a problem unless it is one of the 'feed and weed' type that contains hormone weed-killers. It is unsuitable for using near a pond, because fertiliser will encourage the growth of algae and turn the water green.

How often you mow depends on the time of year, the weather and the type of grass. The golden rule is never to take off more than one-third of the growth at a single mowing. Fine lawns can be cut to leave 1 cm (0.5 in) of grass, and rye grass lawns to leave 2.5 cm (1 in) in summer and 4 cm (1.5 in) in winter. In the summer a rye grass lawn probably needs a weekly cut and a fine grass lawn needs two cuts each week.

Clipping removal

Removing the grass clippings discourages earthworms, lessens the spread of annual meadow grass and gives a better surface finish. However, leaving clippings on a lawn encourages earthworms and improves the soil. Rake off any clumps of clippings or they will kill the grass beneath and encourage fungus diseases. After the first two cuts it is easier to leave the grass box off. Short clippings on the surface soon disappear from the action of worms.

Making it easier

If you have to replace your lawnmower, choose a Mulching Mower. These lawnmowers do not have a grass box. The blades rotate in such a way that the clippings are chopped very small.

Re-seeding

Sowing seeds into an established lawn keeps the grass looking thick and lush. Sow the seeds when the soil is moist and warm enough for rapid germination. You should rake the lawn before sowing and water it afterwards. Bare patches need special treatment and extra seeds.

Moss

Few gardeners can boast a moss-free lawn. Moss looks lush and green in winter but in summer, when you want to use the lawn, it looks dreadful. To add insult to injury, moss kills the fine grasses that are the key to a good lawn.

A lawn can be kept fairly free of moss by spiking it with a garden fork to let air into the soil and improve drainage. (The 'spike sandals' often advertised are ineffective because their spikes are too short.) Leaving the grass box off every second mowing encourages earthworms and they do this work for you, though it takes a little time for the population to build up. A dressing of lime also encourages earthworms – the more earthworms, the more quickly surface clippings disappear. Worm casts look unsightly but are easily spread with a brush. In spring a lawn with lots of worms will attract blackbirds – watch them fill their beaks before flying back to their young.

There is a large range of moss killers to choose from but few different active ingredients. All work fairly well but Armillatox is probably the best

choice. This rather smelly liquid is diluted 200.1 and applied with a watering can. It is longer lasting than others as it kills the spores as well as the growing moss. Armillatox can also be used to keep paths free from moss and algae. The best time to treat a lawn with a moss killer is before you apply the autumn feed.

Making it easier

A gap is often left between the lawn and a hard surface. Both mowing and edging are easier if the lawn is butted to the hard surface. A single pass with this lawn edger keeps the boundary neat and tidy.

Making it easier

1 An electric lawn rake, or a cultivator with a lawn rake attachment, is an easy and effective method for getting rid of thatch and moss. The best type is one in which you push the machine (the motor drives the rake), as it gives better control. Walk quickly for a light raking and slowly for a heavy raking. A second pass at right angles to the first may be necessary for a lawn with lots of moss and thatch.

2 Almost all lawns consist of grass. Camomile lawns are nice in theory but very difficult in practice. An alternative to grass is clover. White clover is green, winter and summer. It needs fewer cuts than grass and is attractive when allowed to flower. Clover flowers attract bees, which may be a disadvantage if grand-children are likely to be using the lawn for play (see p 146).

Trees

A lawn may be enhanced by a single ('specimen') tree. Take care when deciding what tree to buy as, once established, some trees become too large for the site. A weeping willow, for example, will dwarf the average lawn within five or six years. Another problem with the willow (and other trees, too) is drains. If the roots enter a drain, they grow down its length and may block it. Large types of tree must be planted well away from the house and drains.

There are many good reasons for planting trees. A well chosen tree that is correctly sited will enhance a house, provide shade, improve privacy, increase wildlife and bring lasting pleasure.

This liquidambar tree (sweet gum) provides a focal point at the far end of a garden. The autumn colour, which lasts for several weeks, is a bonus.

Liquidambar trees are very similar to some of the acers. If your garden is too cold and windy for fine-leaved acers to flourish, choose a liquidambar. It is easy to distinguish between an acer and a liquidambar: the leaves on an acer are in opposite pairs along the stem whilst liquidambar leaves grow singly on alternate sides of the stem. There are many types of both liquidambars and acers, some large and some small.

In a larger garden, a small group of trees may be better than just one. Three silver birches planted close together are likely to give a better display than a single specimen.

If you only have space for a single tree, and prefer a fruit tree, your choice is more limited. A solitary apple tree will not pollinate unless it is a family tree with three varieties grafted on a single stem. This seems a good idea but considerable expertise is necessary to prevent one variety from growing much larger than the other two. Cutting the vigorous variety back hard stimulates growth and has the opposite of the desired effect.

A Victoria plum is a good choice for a solitary tree, as it is partially self-fertile and easier to manage than an apple. A Victoria plum on a 'Pixi' rootstock remains fairly small. Unfortunately, fruit trees often have more than their fair share of pests and diseases (discussed in Chapter 8).

Buying a tree

Many trees are container grown and can be planted at any time of year. Bare-rooted trees are available only during the dormant period. November is probably the best time to buy these. The roots of a tree are most important; a container tree with roots growing through the drainage holes is best left in the nursery. Such trees often fail to grow well and the roots may not emerge from the compost into the soil. (This is also true of shrubs.) Before buying a container-grown tree, knock the pot off and examine the root ball: if lots of roots are circling around the bottom of the pot, do not buy it.

Bare-rooted trees usually become established more quickly than container-grown ones. Take great care to prevent the roots from drying out during transit to your garden.

Choosing a tree

If the top of a container tree spreads more than three times the diameter of its container, it is out of balance with the roots. Take care not to buy a tree with this imbalance. Look for short, sturdy trees and reject any with long, wispy growths. The main stem should have a clear area at the bottom and be vertical with a strong 'leading' shoot at the top. With all trees it is better to buy small plants, no older than two or three years. Young trees establish better than larger, older ones. You also have the advantage of being able to shape the tree to your liking.

It is easy to tell the age of a young tree. Identify the current year's growth. Find the point where it grew from older wood (this is called a 'girdle scar'); from that point to the next girdle scar is the previous year's growth, and so on. The number of girdle scars along the oldest branch plus one is equal to the age of the tree in years.

Planting a bare-root tree

- Use sharp secateurs to trim the ragged ends of damaged roots.
- Prune back very long roots.
- Dig a hole larger than is needed to take the roots.
- Drive a stake upright into the middle of the hole until it protrudes about 30 cm (1 ft) above the hole.
- Mix well-rotted manure with the soil heap, at the rate of one part manure to four parts soil.
- Sprinkle a handful of bone meal over the pile.
- Put a little soil in the bottom of the hole.
- Offer the tree into the hole and make sure that the soil mark on the tree is level with the soil surface.
- It is important to plant the tree the same depth as it was in the nursery.
- Spread out the roots and begin to fill the hole.
- Give the tree a little jerk up and down to shake soil around the roots.
- Add more soil and gently firm with the sole of your shoe.
- Fill the hole and firm again.
- Fix a tree tie, making sure that the top of the stake does not chafe the stem.

Do not transport a tree with leaves on the roof of a car, because the leaves will dry out. In the summer, hard surfaces such as concrete can become hot enough to damage a tree placed there even temporarily.

Planting a container-grown tree

- Prepare the planting hole as for a bare-root tree but do not drive a stake into the hole.
- Remove the container and tease the roots from the side and bottom of the root ball, removing some of the compost as you go.
- Return some soil to the hole and offer in the tree. Adjust the amount of soil in the hole until the top of the compost is level with the soil surface.
- Fill the hole and firm the new soil with the sole of your shoe.
- Do not apply any pressure to the top of the root ball or you could damage the roots.

As you dig a hole for a tree, the exact position is lost. This may not be important, but if it is, make and use a tree planting board: cut a notch in the centre and at both ends of a spare piece of wood at least 150 cm (5 ft) long.

Place the centre notch of the board against a cane that is marking the required position of the tree. Push a cane into the two end notches. Remove the centre cane and the board, leaving the other two canes in position.

Dig the hole and, using the end canes, return the board to its original position. Offer the tree in with its stem in the centre notch. Fill the hole and remove the board and canes.

If you forget about the tree tie, it will eventually cut into the trunk. This tie has a firm foam wedge to prevent chafing and its stitches are destroyed by light. After about 18 months the stitches give way and the tie drops off.

Staking

For most trees a short stake is better than a long one. The stake is there to prevent the roots from being disturbed when the wind blows. A tree will form a stronger trunk if it is allowed to bend in the wind. A tree's stem is weakened by a stake that stops it bending. A stake driven through the compost of a container-grown tree may damage the root, so drive the stake in at an angle, avoiding the root ball. Where possible, slope the stake towards the prevailing wind. Fix with a tree tie.

Two stakes are supporting this tree because it is on a very windy site. Note that only the base of the tree is supported.

Care after planting

After planting, cut a circle of black plastic (an empty compost bag is ideal) with a slit along a radius. Fit this snugly round the base of the tree. This will prevent weed growth from competing with the tree and help to retain moisture.

Cover the plastic with coarse bark or stones to prevent it being blown away and to improve its appearance.

It is very important that you make sure the tree is well watered during its first summer. In times of drought give it 20 litres (4 gallons) twice a week. After the first year, remove the plastic circle and replace it with an organic mulch about 7.5 cm (3 in) thick. This should provide all the nutrients necessary. If you do not use organic matter, feed the tree with growmore every spring at the rate of 60 g per sq m (2 oz/sq yd).

If rabbits sometimes invade your garden, fit a tree guard to a height of around 60 cm (2 ft). During the winter, rabbits may eat bark from young trees and cause very serious damage.

Training

Ornamental trees may be trained in a similar way to fruit trees (see pp 89 and 90).

This Acer negundo *'Flamingo' has been trained into a large shrub by removing the main stem. The new growth is trimmed back each spring to maintain the required size.*

Making it easier

When removing a large branch, first cut it off a short distance from the trunk.

Make the second cut up against the trunk, cutting the underside first. It is much easier to remove a short piece of wood without damaging the trunk. Cut larger branches off in several stages.

47

Root control bag

The size of a tree can be restricted by planting it in a 'root control bag'. These bags let the small feeding roots into the surrounding soil but prevent them from expanding into large roots. This restricts the size of the tree. Another advantage is that, if you move house, you can take the tree with you! A Christmas tree in a root control bag can be used year after year – provided you water it while it is inside the house and harden it off after Christmas.

A pear tree ('Concorde') planted in a root control bag three years earlier.

Using a root control bag

Dig a hole the same width as the bag but not quite as deep. Place the bag in the hole and shovel a little soil into the bottom of the bag.

Hold the tree in position and fill the hole with soil, spreading the roots out as you do.

Firm the soil around the roots with your foot. Add more soil, leaving 5 cm (2 in) of the bag above soil level.

Use a sloping stake, pointing towards the prevailing wind. Do not drive the stake through the bag, or the roots will grow through the hole.

Chapter 4

Borders

The secret of a good garden is to select plants that suit your soil and climate. Trying to grow plants that require conditions different from those in your garden will cause you unnecessary frustration.

In an established garden it will be obvious which plants succeed and which do not. In a new garden it is a good idea to try different types of plants and then concentrate on the ones that do well and forget the ones that do not.

Most gardens have at least one border, consisting of a group of plants along a boundary. Many borders were inherited from previous owners and received scant attention when the house was purchased there were more important considerations at the time. Retirement is a good time to take an objective look at the borders and adjust them to suit your new situation. There are no hard and fast rules – it is your garden and if the border pleases you, it is right.

A border can be any length, with a width from 30 cm (1 ft) up to 3.5 m (12 ft) or more. All types of plants are suitable for borders, including shrubs, herbaceous, bulbs, biennials and annuals.

Some borders have only one type of plant – annuals or herbaceous, for example. Mixed borders are the most common, the easiest to maintain and the best for year-round interest. Wide borders can accommodate taller plants better than narrow borders. As a rough guide, the tallest plants should be as high as the border is wide. In general, the tallest

An easy-to-maintain border consists of hardy shrubs with a few hardy ground-cover plants between and in front. This border remained virtually untouched for seven years. In the autumn after this photograph was taken, the berberis (top right) was cut hard back.

plants are at the back and the smallest at the front. To get a natural look, though, avoid regimentation by varying the heights throughout, with the odd taller plant, or group of plants, towards the front of the border.

You can plan your borders to take very little time. You can also plan borders that provide lots of opportunity for raising plants, planting bulbs, tending herbaceous plants, collecting seeds and many of the more interesting and rewarding parts of gardening.

Borders are very personal – no two are alike. Many contain plants that have been given by friends and relations. Some plants have

Border along a roadside hedge in a country cottage garden.

sentimental value, especially those that were 'in my grandmother's garden'. Most borders contain mistakes – large plants that do not 'fit in' or very invasive plants that have spread 'everywhere'.

Annual plants make a very colourful boarder as a temporary feature before the area is planted up in autumn with shrubs and herbaceous plants.

It is possible to buy a pre-planned border that comes complete with plants and a planting plan. In my experience these borders seldom work well, because soil and other factors are so varied. Plants in established gardens nearby give you a good indication of which species will succeed.

Mixed plantings consist of:

- Evergreen shrubs to maintain the structure throughout the winter. These also provide shelter and a scratching area for birds in the event of snow.

- Herbaceous plants to give colour and seasonal change.

- Biennials to provide colour at times when there is little elsewhere.

- Bulbs to flower in late winter and spring.

- Bulbs to flower in summer.

Mixed border. This area is subject to waterlogging and the bed was raised to prevent the plants from being drowned in winter. The edge is supported by concrete cascade blocks filled with gritty soil and planted.

- Hardy annuals (often self-sown) to give a natural effect.
- Half-hardy annuals to provide colour from June until the first frost.

Large borders may accommodate the odd small tree for blossom and/or autumn colour. Trees can be positioned to screen other houses or unsightly buildings. A tree planted near a window will give a better screen than one planted further away. Nevertheless, don't plant a large tree near to the house or the drains.

It is very important that you plant new shrubs a good distance apart from each other, with enough space to develop. This is not as easy as it seems: when the shrubs are small, the planting distances look unrealistic. But, before planting, have a look at a mature one and measure its width – yours will be that big one day. However, planting shrubs the correct distance apart will make a new border look very sparse, so fill the spaces with bulbs, biennials and annuals. The area between the shrubs will reduce year by year and in time may disappear altogether.

This spotted laurel is dominating the border. It also shades plants and obscures others beyond. A typical example of a plant in the wrong place.

The same plant after pruning. Pruning has given the plant a new look as well as improving light and visibility. The decision can now be made whether you leave it or remove it.

Tip

When you buy new shrubs or trees, do not be tempted to buy the largest available. Smaller ones with bare roots are not only cheaper, they are also easier to establish. If two trees or shrubs of the same variety, one large and one small, are planted at the same time, the small one often makes better growth and overtakes the larger one.

A plant in the wrong place

Mistakes are often made: a border plant may be too large, too small or the wrong colour. It may be possible to prune a badly placed plant in such a way as to make it acceptable. This is always worth a try; if the pruning fails to achieve its aim, you can remove the plant.

Mistakes can also be corrected by digging up the offending plant. If the plant is to be moved to a new position, do so during its dormant period or late winter for evergreens. Plants that are being discarded can be removed at any time.

After removing the plant, prepare for its replacement by digging over the area. Mix manure or other organic matter with the soil, using the equivalent of a surface layer 10 cm (4 in) deep. A small handful of bone meal mixed with the soil will help a new plant to establish. Do not use bone meal in gardens where foxes visit or they may dig up the plants – use a small amount of super phosphate or organic phosphate instead.

A sack truck is an ideal way to move a plant, as no lifting is involved. You will find it easier to pull the sack truck than push it. This is especially true over rough ground.

If a plant is to be repositioned, prepare its new place before digging it up. When you dig it up, leave as much soil on the root as possible. This will make it heavy – if you do not have a sack truck, put it onto an old compost bag and drag it.

Dividing herbaceous plants

A lawn edger being used to divide a herbaceous plant into several parts.

After a few years, some herbaceous plants will have spread and formed a large clump. Autumn is a good time to correct this. Use a garden fork to dig up a section at a time and drag the plants clear of the border. Dig over the area, fork in some manure and rake it level. Use a sharp lawn-edging tool or spade to cut the clump into pieces. Each piece should contain several shoots, rosettes or buds. Discard the parts from the middle of the clump and replant three or five of the pieces from the outside of the clump in the old position. Planting odd numbers, rather than even, creates a more natural look.

An alternative way to divide a clump is to use two forks back to back. This method works well only if the handles of the forks are forced together before being pulled apart. Pushing the handles together prises apart the tangled roots at the bottom of the clump.

Hardy annuals

A bare patch in a flower border in spring is easily filled by sowing a few hardy annuals. Hardy annuals are cheap and cheerful, and they also produce a free supply of seeds for the following year.

- Sow in an irregular drift, but use straight lines within the drift.

- Draw drills 15 cm (6 in) apart with an onion hoe.

- Water the bottom of the drills.

- Sow the seeds thinly and cover with multipurpose compost.

- Thin out the seedlings as soon as they are large enough to handle.

As the plants grow, the straight lines disappear. A good time to sow is in the period two or three weeks before and two or three weeks after the date of the last expected frost.

What to plant

Take care with colours. Here, the lupin has been selected to complement the other border plants. A very bright colour is best at the far end of a border. Oranges and pinks are likely to clash. If in doubt, choose white – it goes with any colour!

Common herbaceous plants such as delphiniums and lupins are excellent and, if dead-headed, will flower again. They are also easily raised from seed. Sow in May and pot on in stages to 15 cm (6 in) pots. Plant out in the autumn while the soil is still warm. Place them in groups of three, five or seven plants to get the best effect.

It is a good idea to use mostly common plants – they are common because they are good. Hardy perennials such as lupins can also be grown in large pots. These are useful to fill a temporary gap in the border – don't forget to water them.

A few uncommon plants add interest and create a talking point.

Arum italicum 'Marmoratum'. The photograph of the berries was taken in September, and the leaves in December.

An unusual plant that is easy to grow is *Arum italicum* 'Marmoratum'. The flowers are hidden by the attractive leaves, which grow in early winter and last until the following August. The leaves fall to reveal the remains of the flowers – stems covered in green berries. By September the berries are bright red and there they stay until the new leaves appear in November. A brilliant splash of autumn colour and beautiful foliage in winter.

Borders can also provide flowers for the house. In the summer it is often quite easy to remove a bunch of flowers without spoiling the border. In the winter a few twigs of forsythia, cut five or six

54

weeks before normal flowering time and placed in a vase of water, will soon open into a mass of yellow flowers. Winter jasmine can be treated in a similar way.

Border plants make fewer demands on the soil than vegetables. For the best results, though, some feeding is necessary.

A dark spot in a border can be brightened up by cutting a few flowers and putting them in an old watering can. Small additions to a garden can make a big difference; an empty champagne bottle on a garden table, for example, creates a certain atmosphere.

Feeding

Border plants are healthier and look better if you give the soil an annual mulch. A 5 cm (2 in) layer of rotted manure or garden compost spread over the soil is all that is required. The mulch gradually disappears as the worms pull it into the soil. On most soils a regular mulch makes fertilisers unnecessary. Fertiliser is helpful on an impoverished soil

– especially where builders have removed some of the topsoil. If a fertiliser is needed, choose a complete one such as Chase organic fertiliser, spread at the rate of 60 g per sq m (2 oz/sq yd) between the border plants, in spring. A handful of bone meal mixed into the soil before planting a shrub is beneficial, as it slowly releases phosphate into the soil. A foliar feed of seaweed extract in the spring is a good way to insure against deficiencies in trace elements. Don't splash the blooms, or you may stain the petals.

Weeds

A Dutch hoe is an effective tool to control seedling weeds growing between plants. Use it on a dry day when the weeds are very small: keep the blade on the surface, taking care not to disturb more than the top centimetre (0.5 in) of soil. Going deeper is likely to damage plant roots and cause more weed seeds to germinate.

A properly maintained mixed border requires very little weeding, especially if all weeds are removed before they shed seed. Sadly, some borders contain perennial weeds that can be difficult to eradicate. An annual mulch helps to control seedling weeds but has no effect on perennial weeds, which have energy reserves in underground parts. A mulch can also make matters worse: imported manure or your own garden compost may contain weed seeds.

Making it easier

Hand weeding is much easier from a kneeler. The side supports help you to get down and up, as well as increasing your reach into the border.

Couch grass, convolvulus (bindweed), nettles and other perennial weeds must be removed as soon as you see them; otherwise, they will spread and become invasive. Use a fork and get out all of the underground parts or they will regrow.

Free-seeding flowers, such as poppies, can become a nuisance. Remove the dead flower heads before they shed their seeds. Save a few to ripen indoors; sprinkle seed from these, in appropriate areas of the border, where they will flower the following year.

Using glyphosate

Perennial weeds (with the exception of horsetails) can be controlled by using glyphosate weed-killer (sold as Roundup and Tumbleweed). This chemical will also kill border plants, so use it with extreme care. Glyphosate is absorbed by plant leaves and is said to be broken down to harmless substances on reaching the soil (there

are doubts about the accuracy of this statement). The chemical moves throughout the plant and, after two or three weeks, the whole plant dies – including the underground parts. Glyphosate only works well on weeds that are actively growing, especially those with plenty of leaves to absorb the chemical. It is a very useful substance to clear a neglected patch of ground. Spray it on during periods of active growth and three weeks later the weeds will be dead.

Invasive weeds, such as couch grass, are almost impossible to control in borders and rockeries by using a hoe. A successful method is to have a small quantity of diluted glyphosate in a bucket. Put on rubber gloves and pull a woollen glove over one hand. Dip the fingers of the woollen glove into the solution and wet as many weed leaves as possible.

Convolvulus is very difficult to get rid of, because it twines around the plants. If it is growing in a shrub, I find that the best method is to insert several canes at an angle away from the shrub. Train some of the weed shoots along the canes and, when they reach the top, cover the shrub with a plastic sheet and spray the convolvulus. Leave the canes in position until the weed has died.

Support

Staking border plants is very important. The time to stake a plant is *before* it needs it! Staking a plant after it has fallen is less successful, as the top has usually changed direction. There is also the possibility of the stem breaking.

There are lots of different methods of staking, many of which are quite expensive.

A link stake consists of a plastic-coated steel rod, with a ring and a hook. Three or more stakes are pushed into the ground and hooked together to encircle a plant. They are easily unhooked to accommodate the odd shoot that grows outside the support. Link stakes are available in different sizes and last for years.

Some supports on the market consist of grids through which plants grow. These give good support, as the stems that grow through hold each other up. However, grids are seldom large enough to cover the whole plant. Stems that miss the grid should be tied to it with string.

Without doubt the most versatile, and cost effective, method of supporting plants is bamboo canes and string. To support a herbaceous plant, push four or five bamboo canes firmly into the soil round its perimeter. Tie two circles of string round at different heights. A danger with this method is the possibility of eye injury when you bend over an unseen cane. To prevent this, fit a cane cap on each cane – which also makes them more obvious.

Maintaining a mixed border

Spring

Your border should be a mass of colour for months, with spring bulbs, pansies, daises, forget-me-nots. Early colour gradually gives way to the biennials such as foxgloves and wallflowers, early flowering herbaceous plants, aquilegias, verbascums and pyrethrums. Your main jobs are dead-heading and arranging supports for the herbaceous plants

(which will be getting bigger every day), sowing hardy annuals and controlling weeds.

As spring gives way to summer it is time to plant the half-hardy annuals that so often replace the spring bulbs. There may still be lots of foliage, but this will be feeding the bulbs for next year's flowers, so leave it until the leaves are turning yellow. Then cut the leaves off at ground level. Plant annuals in the same place: this is far easier than lifting and storing the bulbs.

Making it easier

A better method is to plant your bulbs in permeable woven plastic (eg Gropax) bags buried in the soil. When it is time to put in the bedding plants, lift out the bags, complete with bulbs, and stand them out of the way (alongside a shed, for example). Water them and give a little feed to swell the bulbs. When the leaves are completely dead, the bulbs can be stored in the dark until planting time in the autumn.

Summer

Spaces in front of and between shrubs are ideal places for half-hardy annuals.

Plant half-hardy annuals and perennials. Water in dry weather and continue dead-heading. There will be plenty of time to enjoy your garden – and visit others.

Autumn

When the first frosts have finally killed off your late-summer-flowering plants your borders will need a big tidy-up. Cut down dead flowers and foliage – not too low, though; leave the bottom few inches to protect the buds below from winter weather. Pull up all dead annuals and biennials. Remove, divide and replant any herbaceous plants that are becoming too large. Cut back shrubs where necessary. This is quite a long list; it is also an enjoyable way of spending a few sunny afternoons outside.

Winter

Shake snow off evergreen shrubs to prevent the branches from breaking.

Feed the birds on the ground as well as on the bird table. Keep off the lawns and borders, and enjoy the winter scenes.

Making it easier

Both secateurs and loppers are available with a ratchet action. These sever thick, hard stems with almost no effort. When using ratchet loppers, hold one handle stationary and 'pump' the other.

It is possible to purchase the type of trolley used in garden centres. In some circumstances this type of trolley may be more suitable than a wheelbarrow. For example, it can be loaded in such a way that downward pressure on the handles, rather than upward, is needed. You may find that pressing down is easier than lifting.

In larger gardens a wheelbarrow is essential. A barrow with two wheels is easier to balance but not quite so easy to manoeuvre.

The dry bog

A dry bog is a way to grow water-loving plants in a bed of gravel. The gravel is held in a waterproof lining, containing sufficient water to keep the plants well supplied. Each plant has its own compost root ball surrounded by the gravel.

A dry bog can be any size or shape – it fits into a small garden as easily as into a large one. Preparing a dry bog is time consuming but it is a once-and-for-all job and, when completed, you can relax and enjoy it for years.

Arrange the plants before planting, to make sure you are happy with the way they look. Then scrape a hole in the gravel until you reach water. Remove the pot, place the plant in the hole and fill it up with gravel.

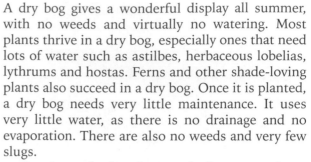

A dry bog gives a wonderful display all summer, with no weeds and virtually no watering. Most plants thrive in a dry bog, especially ones that need lots of water such as astilbes, herbaceous lobelias, lythrums and hostas. Ferns and other shade-loving plants also succeed in a dry bog. Once it is planted, a dry bog needs very little maintenance. It uses very little water, as there is no drainage and no evaporation. There are also no weeds and very few slugs.

Creating a dry bog is very similar to creating a garden pond. It consists of a flat-bottomed hole, 25 cm (10 in) deep, fitted with a pond liner and filled with coarse, sand-free gravel instead of water. There is some water – 10 cm (4 in) in the bottom. Pot-grown plants are removed from their pots and sunk in the gravel so that the base of the root ball is in contact with the water. The only problem is staking – a stake pushed in further than the 25 cm (10 in) depth will puncture the lining and release the water. If you construct a dry bog, don't include very tall plants in the planting scheme!

If you worry about your grandchildren falling into the garden pond, consider converting it into a dry bog. Simply fill it with gravel instead of water and

▲ Dry bog in April. This dry bog is at the end of a border and forms an integral part of it.

The same dry bog in June.

plant it up. Before filling it in, pull down one corner of the pond liner 7.5 cm (5 in) to allow excess water to drain away. You should also protect the pond liner by lining it with old compost bags, or similar, before tipping in the gravel.

Never be in a hurry to remove dead stems. Late autumn sunshine on this border is very attractive. On frosty mornings the border has additional charm.

Camellia and other early-spring-flowering shrubs give a much better display if they are fertilised and watered the previous August when the flower buds are beginning to form. Camellias are less likely to be damaged by frost if they are shaded from early morning sunshine.

If you are concerned about security around your home, a pyracantha is a good shrub to have by a vulnerable window or downpipe – it has vicious thorns. The June flowers encourage wildlife and look better than a burglar alarm. The bright red berries in autumn give months of pleasure. There is also the pleasure of watching thrushes enjoy a winter feed as they strip off the berries.

If where you live has a pleasant view, take care not to block it out with large garden structures or plants.

Houttuynia cordata (sorry, no common name) spreads in a similar way to couch grass. The growth is often sparse, producing a poor display. This one is planted in a 22 cm (9 in) bottomless pot and sunk in the soil. It gives a striking display throughout the summer and autumn.

Roses must be positioned with extra care, because they do not fit easily into a mixed border. Large gardens may have the luxury of a separate rose bed, with standards complementing the bush roses below. A climber on a wall, or over an arch, is possible in many smaller gardens, adding height in a delightful way.

Roses are deep rooted and require a deep soil, preferably one well supplied with organic matter. Roses do well in clay soils; they will also do well in sandy soils if a good mulch is applied each year.

Roses

Roses are the most popular and widely grown species in the world. The growth form is very varied, and there can be few gardens that do not include at least one rose. They range from the miniature pot rose, easily grown from seed, to the prolific rambler filling lots of space with colour, scent and large red hips.

Planting a bare-root rose

- The site should be in good light and away from harsh draughts.
- Mix a handful of bone meal with 10 litres (2 gallons) of coir.
- Dig out a hole, large and deep enough to accommodate the roots.
- Mix the coir with the dug out soil and put a little into the hole.
- Trim any damaged roots with sharp secateurs.
- Identify the bud union (where the bottom branches join the stem).
- Place a cane across the hole and position the rose with the bud union 5 cm (2 in) below the level of the cane.
- Remove the cane and spread the roots into their natural position.
- Fill the hole, and give the bush a sharp jerk to shake the soil around the roots.
- Firm down gently with the sole of your shoe and top up with more soil.
- Prune all the branches hard, leaving them 10–15 cm (4–6 in) long.
- Apply 5 litres (1 gallon) of water.
- Cover the soil with an organic mulch.

Pruning

Regular pruning is essential to keep the plants within bounds and to encourage flowering. There is no mystique about pruning roses: it is very easy. Bush roses on a very windy site will have less 'wind rock' if a third of the year's growth is removed in the autumn.

Pruning a bush rose

- Use sharp secateurs or loppers.
- Choose a sunny, windless day in winter.
- Do not bother about pruning to 'outward-facing buds'.
- Remove any dead or diseased wood.
- Cut the oldest branch off at the base.
- Cut all remaining branches down by half.
- Leave thin, twiggy stems untouched.

Making it easier

Prune by using a light electric hedge trimmer and reduce the height of each bush by a little more than half. Tests have shown this method to be as effective as pruning with secateurs.

Training a climber

Upright growths flower at the top, leaving bare stems below. Horizontal stems produce flower shoots all along the length and give a good display from the ground up. The aim of training is to prevent upright stems and keep others as near to the horizontal as possible. Although the new growth is green and pliable, it is likely to break off at the base. Take extreme care and bend new growth into a near-horizontal position and tie to a trellis or to 'vine eyes' in a wall.

Where a climbing rose is growing up a pillar, the stems should be trained to spiral the pillar.

Dead-heading

Dead-heading greatly increases the number of flowers. To dead-head, break the dying flowers off at a point just below the flower – the base of what would become the hip. This method is far more effective than the one that is usually recommended – using secateurs to cut back to the next true leaf.

Feeding

A mulch of around 7.5 cm (3 in) of well-rotted stable or farmyard manure applied every autumn will supply a rose with all the necessary nutrients. On poor soils, apply a rose fertiliser once in spring and once in summer according to the manufacturer's instructions.

Watering

Roses are deep rooted and, once established, only need watering in very dry weather.

Diseases

When you buy roses, select varieties that are resistant to disease. Rake up fallen leaves, especially any showing signs of black spot (see 'Fungus diseases' on p 129).

Sweet peas

The sweet pea is the most popular annual climber for both cut flowers and a garden display. Enthusiasts sow the seeds in October and grow them slowly in cold conditions. For general garden use – up a wigwam or against a trellis or fence – plants from a February sowing are easier to grow and almost as effective.

Sow seeds, 3 cm (1 in) deep, individually in deep Rootrainers or sweet pea tubes filled with moist multipurpose compost. There is no need to chip the seeds (cut a little of the seed coat away) – it is a difficult job that often leads to cut fingers. Place them in a propagator or warm room. As soon as the shoots begin to emerge, transfer them to a cold frame or cold greenhouse. Ventilate whenever possible to keep the temperature as low as possible but don't allow them to freeze; growth will be slow but that is an advantage. When two leaves are fully expanded, pinch out the growing point – this is an essential procedure, as strong side shoots replace the weak main stem.

Sweet peas perform best in deep soil that has been well manured. Transplant to the flowering position early in April. Protect the plants from wind with fleece and push in a few short twiggy sticks for the plants to climb to the trellis or other support. The plants seem to make very little progress for several weeks as the roots develop. Later, growth is very rapid and you will be rewarded with masses of flowers. Sweet peas must be dead-headed regularly or they set seeds and the flowers stop. Dead-head as soon as the lowest bloom on the flower stem fades; the plants will respond by producing more flowers.

The sweet pea is ideal to encourage grandchildren to take an interest in the garden.

Chapter 5

On the Patio

The dictionary definition of a patio is 'a paved outside area adjoining a house'. The modern patio is much more than that; it is an integral part of the home with many uses including sitting, eating and entertaining. The patio is also an integral part of the garden, presenting different ways of growing and enjoying plants. Containers, baskets, socks and pouches all have a place on the patio.

Where a patio includes a fence or a wall, it may be better to make a hole in the patio and plant in the soil beneath. This Solanum crispum *needs very little attention apart from trimming back in late autumn to prevent it from becoming too large.*

This patio is at the back of an old cottage. It is 3 metres (13 ft) wide and 7 metres (23 ft) long, surrounded by a high brick wall. The wall is painted white to increase the light. With its raised beds, baskets, containers and pots, it is full of year-round interest and a very pleasant place to be. ▼

Containers

Plastic containers filled with soil-less compost have the advantage of being light enough to be moved around. They can be planted up and grown on in one part of the garden and moved to the patio when in full colour. Stone and terracotta containers are best left in one spot. They can be permanently planted with shrubs or planted with annuals in summer and bulbs for a spring display. A container can be organised to hold a number of individual pots. This allows you to make regular changes in the display – for example, taking out a pot of dying daffodils and replacing it with a pot of tulips that are coming into bud.

Almost any plant can be grown in a container. Permanent plantings in containers should be in a loam-based compost – preferably a John Innes type. This lasts longer than a soil-less compost; it is also much heavier, so the container is less likely to blow over.

All permanent-planted containers should be stood on pot 'feet' or thin wooden blocks. This will prevent the drainage holes from becoming blocked and worms entering the compost.

If container plants are to remain vigorous and healthy, they must be watered and fed correctly. Feed during periods of active growth; not too much

nitrate, some phosphate and a little additional potash for flowers and fruit. Reduce watering in winter to a minimum but do not allow the compost to dry out completely. Take care not to allow the compost to freeze solid; many otherwise hardy plants cannot withstand frozen roots. Wrapping the container with a few layers of bubble plastic or hessian may keep its temperature above freezing. Nevertheless, even well-wrapped pots might freeze if the temperature remains below freezing for several days and nights.

Making it easier

Castors on which conservatory and patio plants can be mounted are available in garden centres. This makes it much easier to move the plants for cleaning or to change the display. You could possibly make your own with a few pieces of wood and four castors.

It is easy to have a good patio display by grouping pots together. This allows you to make changes throughout the seasons. The plants in this summer display include a number that are half hardy. The half-hardy plants will be moved to the greenhouse for winter. If you live in a mild part of the country, the cordyline (the tall one with upright, spiky leaves) might survive outside. If the weather becomes very wet, tie the leaves upright into a loose cylinder with the tips together to shed rain. If hard frost is forecast, wrap a piece of hessian round the whole plant.

Autumn containers will give months of colour. This 30 cm (12 in) pot contains seven varieties: viola, pansy, cyclamen, sedum, helichrysum, lamium and thyme.

Other plants suitable for autumn containers include: ivies, campanula, ajuga, Solanum 'Ballon', santolina, origanum, lysimachia, mint and other herbs – especially ones with coloured leaves such as tricoloured sage.

A little humour is not out of place on the patio.

A pebble pool makes an interesting feature, with the sound of running water and a drink for the birds.

The container adds interest to this sanvitalia (creeping zinnia), a half-hardy annual sown in March to flower from June to October.

Some containers have a very small drainage hole that may become blocked. Prevent this by placing a layer of coarse material in the bottom such as chunks of broken poly-styrene from old packaging. If the container is at risk from being blown over, use broken brick or very coarse gravel instead.

This large bougainvillea was bought as a small pot plant with the main growth curled into a circle. The plant was potted on and the stems carefully unwound and trained upwards. It is kept in a frost-free green-house during the winter and stands on a sunny patio throughout the summer.

A few sunflower seeds sown in a container will grow into a delightful display for a few weeks. Make sure that you sow a dwarf variety – this one is 'Pacino'.

Trailing geraniums

There are many novel ways of displaying plants. Trailing geraniums make a barrel of colour that is easily made and easily maintained.

1 Get a large, cheap water butt or other plastic container. This one was once filled with orange juice! Cut holes in the sides 5 cm (2 in) diameter about 30 cm (12 in) apart. Place the container in its final position before putting a few bricks in the bottom to prevent it from blowing over.

2 Fill the bin up to the bottom holes with sharp sand (concreting sand). This helps both drainage and water retention.

3 Fill the centre with an old plastic container and a large plant pot. This saves compost and helps to distribute water to the roots.

4 Starting at the bottom, plant one trailing geranium in each hole, filling in with compost as you go. The tub will need less maintenance if you add water-retaining crystals and

slow-release fertiliser to the compost. Plug each hole with a moss substitute to retain the compost. Plant three geraniums in the top, near to the edge.

Hanging baskets

Hanging baskets transform a dull wall.

Buying a basket

There are many different types of hanging baskets and it is important to get the right one. Things to consider include:

- Volume – a basket that is shaped to hold a lot of compost is best. Avoid flat-bottomed and shallow baskets.

- A basket 35 cm (14 in) across is the optimum size for mixed plantings; a 30 cm (12 in) basket is a bit small, as it dries out fairly quickly; and a 40 cm (16 in) one is possibly too heavy for the bracket – and the gardener.

- Open sides increase the planting area and make a better show. The down-side is that this type needs a liner.

- A shallow well in the bottom helps to retain water without producing a waterlogged area.

- Protruding 'pegs' on the base enable it to stand level while you are filling it.

- A rim 5 cm (2 in) deep round the top makes watering much easier.

- A wire or thin plastic rim round the top sometimes cuts plant stems – you can easily prevent this by wrapping it with a moss substitute.

A Security basket is a good buy because:
- *it comes complete with a bracket;*
- *it is made of plastic-coated wrought iron;*
- *it is easily turned round to show the best side;*
- *it does not swing about in the wind;*
- *you do not have to reach as high when hanging it up;*
- *there are no chains to get in the way when you are filling or emptying the basket;*
- *the hole at the base will take a small padlock.*

Basket liners

Although natural sphagnum moss makes a good liner, it is best left where it belongs – in the countryside. There are several other materials available, from papier mâché to various felts. The best one I have found is Woolmoss: it is easy and effective in use and looks good. The only disadvantage is that our birds take it to line their nests. This is partially remedied by tying some onto the bird table.

Basket compost

Soil-based composts are too heavy for hanging baskets. Use a good multipurpose soil-less compost. Mix in slow-release fertiliser and a water-holding gel with the compost before using it. Add only the amounts recommended, as too much of either can be disastrous.

Summer baskets are best planted up in late April and grown on in a greenhouse. They must be hardened off before being left outside permanently. If you do not have a greenhouse, plant the basket four weeks later with plants that have been hardened off.

Planting up a hanging basket

- Add a carefully measured amount of water-retaining crystals to a top-quality soil-less compost.
- Add the recommended amount of slow-release fertiliser to the compost.
- Put a circle of black plastic sheet in the bottom to create a well about 2 cm (1 in) deep.
- Line the bottom half of the basket with Woolmoss.
- Half fill the basket with compost.
- If the basket is to hang against a wall, decide which side will be showing.
- Insert five or six trailing plants through the basket sides, with the roots in contact with the compost.
- Line the upper half of the basket.
- Position any tall-growing plant in the back of the basket. The top of its root ball should be about 2 cm (1 in) below the top of the basket.
- Arrange the other plants in the top of the basket. These plants should be in upright positions – the trailers will trail as they grow.
- Fill the spaces between the root balls, packing the compost in fairly firmly.
- Check that there are no spaces; check also that the top of the compost is 2 cm (1 in) below the basket rim.
- Cover the surface with moss (raked from the lawn).
- Water thoroughly.

Plants for hanging baskets

Wherever possible, use Rootrainer-grown plants for hanging baskets. The long roots fit through the side of the basket and make good contact with the compost.

Summer baskets should be in full flower for four months. Your choice of plants is very important, as many otherwise suitable plants have short flowering periods. You also need to keep the amount of dead-heading to a minimum.

Foliage plants – Swedish ivy (*Plectranthus*) and helichrysum, for example – are no problem because they are included for their leaves, not flowers. Both are easily grown from cuttings.

Basket plants from seed

Trailing lobelia *Sow in early February and prick out into 'Rannoch' Rootrainers. It is excellent for planting through the side of a basket; it soon covers a large area and becomes a mass of colour. Lobelia tends to die out in August, by which time the space is covered with trailers from above.* cont'd

Impatiens (Busy Lizzie) Sow in February and prick out into 7.5 cm (3 in) pots. Busy Lizzies are one of the brightest and best basket plants. Plant them through the sides and in the top of the basket. They can be used for single-species baskets where they form a large sphere of colour. Good for shady places.

Bidens Sow in February. Plants from seed are less prolific than those from cuttings but they are a good yellow and very free flowering. Plant only one or two in each basket, because the roots are aggressive.

Sanvitalia Sow in February and prick out into 'Shrub' Rootrainers. They produce a mass of small yellow flowers all summer. This plant is a spreader rather than a trailer.

Nolana Sow in March. This is a good trailer with attractive blue trumpets and a long flowering period.

Surfinia petunia Sow in September from home-saved seeds. Over-winter the plants in frost-free conditions and then propagate from cuttings in the spring. The surfinia is very free flowering, trails well and lasts throughout the life of the basket.

Petunias Sow in March. Petunias have a better choice of colours than surfinia but are not as reliable or as tolerant of rain.

Begonias (tuberous rooted) These are very reliable with masses of large, colourful flowers plus attractive leaves. Seeds are expensive; they need to be sown early in the year and are not very easy. It is probably better to buy plugs or tubers.

Making it easier

If you have problems growing impatiens from seed (they can be difficult), buy plug plants in March and grow them on in 'Shrub' Rootrainers.

Basket plants from cuttings

Scaevola (fan flower) Cuttings are very difficult to root, so it is probably better to buy them as plugs. Available in blue and white, scaevola is one of the best basket plants, with a mass of trailing colour throughout the life of the basket.

Trailing fuchsias These are excellent for the top of the basket but several of the varieties will set seed and stop flowering after a few weeks when in basket conditions.

Fuschia (thalia) This does not trail but is a good choice for the top of a basket. Put it near the back and plant trailers of other varieties in front.

Single trailing pelargoniums (often called geraniums) Buy one plant early in January, and keep it warm, watered and fed. Take the new growth as cuttings as soon as it is large enough (see p 25). You should get two or three lots of cuttings up to and including early May. The pelargonium is one of the easiest and best basket plants, and not as likely to suffer from drought as most of the others. The flowers last a long time, so very little dead-heading is required.

Double nasturtiums are good basket and container plants. Unlike their single relatives, they do not set seed. They have to be grown from cuttings, but fortunately these root very easily. Take a few cuttings during the summer and keep them frost-free all winter. The following spring these new plants will produce masses of cuttings in plenty of time to grow into displays similar to the one shown here.

There are, of course, many other suitable plants. I have mentioned only some of my favourites.

Tip

Hanging baskets that became a little neglected during a holiday can often be restored by immersing them in water until the bubbles stop. When the plants are recovering, give a weak feed plus a little seaweed extract. Your reward will be two more months of pleasure for a little extra care.

Caring for hanging baskets

Hanging baskets need daily watering – even in wet weather. Water-retaining crystals help to increase water capacity but they make no difference to the amount of water the plants use. If slow-release fertilisers were not included in the compost, a weekly feed is necessary as well. Choose a general-purpose fertiliser that is high in potash (K).

Making it easier

Hanging baskets can be difficult to water. A basket in a wrought iron hoop presents no difficulty and is a delightful item to stand on the patio.

Where there is a tap nearby, this watering system works well but, if your water pressure is high, do not turn the tap fully on. An easy-to-use on/off switch is operated by a trigger.

Note Outside taps must, by law, be fitted with an anti-flowback device.

Tip

Flower pouches add colour to a fence or wall. Sometimes the wet compost is too heavy for the plastic handle. Spread the load with a short length of garden cane.

Lewisia plants are very hardy but quickly rot off in winter if the crown becomes filled with water. Planting in a garden sock will overcome the problem. The plants shown here were raised in a cold greenhouse from seeds sown in April. In September they were planted into a garden sock filled with multipurpose compost and hung on an outside wall. They flowered throughout the following May and June and, with a little feeding and care, will flower at the same time every year. A garden sock is more durable than a flower pouch and much easier to water.

Food from the patio

The patio need not be confined to flowers. It is fun to grow some of your own food in pots and containers. Some food plants are also quite attractive; several of the common herbs have variegated forms and the flowers are attractive to bees and butterflies. Carrot foliage is delicate and there are lettuce varieties that add colour as well as interest. There is nothing particularly attractive about potato foliage but a few early potatoes from a container have a flavour that surpasses any bought ones. For the best results, food plants must have full sun – you will be disappointed if you try to grow them out of sight in shady places.

Beans

Broad beans in a
plastic container.

Broad beans grown in a container produce a small crop. Dwarf French beans are much better suited to container production; the yield is large, especially when harvested regularly. 'Ferrari' is possibly the best variety for container production. Runner beans need an enormous amount of water and are not very suitable for containers. The dwarf varieties are more likely to succeed than the climbers, and are certainly less likely to blow over.

Carrots

One of the most
worthwhile container
crops is carrots.

As well as being tasty, carrots are easy to grow and the crop is enormous. All you need is a container, some multipurpose compost and a packet of seeds. The container can be any size or shape. Make sure that it is not too heavy to lift when filled with wet compost. This container is 84 cm (33 in) long and 28 cm (11 in) wide and provides masses of carrots for 12 weeks or more. It is made of polystyrene but that is not important. What *is* important is the depth, which needs to be around 15 cm (6 in). Stump-rooted varieties are ideal for containers; 'Amsterdam Forcing' and 'Early Scarlet Horn' are my favourites. Do not bother growing the small round varieties, as the yield is too low.

Make sure that your container has drainage holes and then fill it with multipurpose compost. Use a rose can to thoroughly wet the compost.

Sow seeds of a stump-rooted variety very thinly over the whole surface and cover with a thin layer of vermiculite.

Keep the container in a light place. A greenhouse or conservatory is ideal until May. From May until the end of July they will germinate outside on the patio. *When the seedlings appear, thin them to about 1 cm (0.5 in) apart.*

Water as necessary, directly onto the compost and not over the foliage.

Start pulling the carrots as soon as they are large enough. Pull the big ones first and leave the others to grow. Remove the tops immediately after you harvest them or they will draw water from the roots, making them soft. With a clean container and fresh compost you are unlikely to get any pest or disease problems – except for carrot fly. If you are unlucky enough to have carrot fly in your area, construct a fleece barrier 60 cm (2 ft) high around the container. (Make a wooden frame – tile laths are ideal – with fleece held by staples or drawing pins.) There is no need to cover the top.

Salads

Lettuce and rocket

Raise these from seed on the windowsill or in the greenhouse and then plant them into containers. With the exception of 'Little Gem', the loose leaf varieties are best for containers. Sprinkle a few rocket seeds between the lettuce plants a week after you transplant them. Harvest the rocket by picking the leaves as required, and pull them up as soon as they run to seed.

Chervil

Sow this in a small container and harvest regularly – the leaves are attractive and have a taste of aniseed.

Salad or spring onions

Salad or spring onions can be grown in a similar way to carrots, described above. Sow in April and again in late May. Spring onions are slow to germinate and the foliage is not very attractive.

Potatoes

You need a bucket-shaped container with drainage holes and a capacity of at least 15 litres (3 gallons). In January buy a few seed potatoes – they must be an early variety ('Swift', 'Maris Bard' or 'Rocket', for example). Put them on a tray with the buds uppermost. Place the tray in a well-lit, frost-free windowsill and short, strong, green shoots will emerge.

Put 15 cm (6 in) of multipurpose compost into the bottom of the container and place two tubers, buds upwards, on top. Cover with 7.5 cm (3 in) of compost, and water. As the shoots grow, add old growing-bag or garden compost until the container is almost full. Don't bury all the shoots, and always leave some leaves in the light. Water regularly and feed with a tomato feed six weeks after planting. Feed again two weeks later. Take care not to allow the compost to dry out – feeling the weight of the container is a good test for moisture content.

Note 'Potato tubs' are available. These are best for late potatoes but I feel that they are not very good value for money.

Herbs

There are very many different herbs and, where space is limited, there is little point in growing most of them. Grow only the ones you will use – thyme, rosemary and sage are shrubby perennials and ideal plants for containers as well as being useful in the kitchen. Chive is another perennial that succeeds in a patio container; it has useful leaves and attractive flowers. A container of moss curled parsley on the patio is attractive as well as being useful. (See page 109 for the best way to grow parsley.)

The foliage can be supported with four canes (fitted with cane caps) pushed inside the rim supporting two horizontal circles of string. Or you can allow the stems to fall on the floor. After the plants have flowered or after 12 weeks, whichever is the sooner, harvest the potatoes by pulling up one of the plants; if that does not provide sufficient for your immediate needs, empty the container. The sooner they are cooked the better they will taste.

Mint is easy to grow from its underground stems (rhizomes). Fill a container to within 7.5 cm (3 in) of the rim. Place a few short lengths of mint rhizomes on the surface, add 5 cm (2 in) more compost and water. The shoots will be large enough to harvest in a few weeks. You can remove the flower buds to encourage more leaves or leave them to flower. The blue flowers are attractive to a whole range of insects. After the second year the mint will only be growing around the edge of the container. Empty it out, save a few rhizomes and start again – with fresh compost.

Herbs can also be grown in a garden sock or flower pouch and hung on a south-facing wall.

Making it easier

An easy way to grow herbs is to buy growing ones from a supermarket. You will find that these consist of a group of overgrown seedlings. Split them up into small bunches. Fill a garden sock with multipurpose compost and plant through holes made in the side of the sock.

This pot has a wick in the bottom, which allows water to feed slowly into the sock. This prevents the water from running out of the top planting holes.

Chapter 6

Fruit

Strawberries

Retirement is a good time to plant fruit trees and bushes. Bushes (eg blackcurrants) and canes (eg raspberries) fruit in the second year after planting. Trees on modern root stocks are small, easily cared for and begin regular cropping within two or three years of planting.

Fruit gives an excellent return from a small space. It does, however, need a permanent area and a little know-how. The basic principles are very easy, and growing fruit is a rewarding experience.

Most soils will grow fruit trees and bushes. Freedom from waterlogging and plenty of humus are the only requirements. It is possible to grow fruit in a waterlogged area by constructing a raised bed and planting in that (see pp 8 and 9). As fruit is a long-term crop, it is worth taking time and care over soil preparation. For best results, your soil needs to be very slightly acid (pH 6.5). The year before planting, treat acid soils with lime. Alkaline soil is more difficult, but you can lower the pH by treating it with ground sulphur. This is rather expensive but less so if you confine the treatment to the trees' root zones. The soil should be deeply worked and a heavy dressing of well-rotted manure mixed in.

A site in full sun, with some shelter from strong winds, is ideal. Make sure your site is free from all perennial weeds. If you are unable to avoid a frost pocket or hollow, select late-flowering varieties.

Exotic fruits, such as kiwi, are advertised in catalogues as easy to grow. In my experience it is far better to grow the common soft and top fruits and treat the exotics as a bit of fun – if you have the space.

A strawberry plant will produce a good yield for three or four years, after which time it becomes diseased and should be discarded. Start again in a new bed, in another part of the garden. Soil in which potatoes were grown the previous year is unsuitable. When establishing a strawberry bed buy new, certified plants. An alternative way to grow strawberries is in patio containers and strawberry tubs.

If you have a greenhouse, a strawberry bed will give you a bonus in the form of runners for forcing (see p 33).

There are lots of varieties to choose from. My favourites are 'Emily' for an early crop and 'Rhapsody' for a later one. Perpetual flowering varieties are best confined to containers or tubs.

Planting

Autumn is the best time to plant, although planting can continue until the end of March. Cold-stored runners are available for summer planting.

Strawberries need planting as soon as they arrive. Plant them 38 cm (15 in) apart, in rows 75 cm (30 in) apart. Make a hole with a trowel, large enough to take the roots. Spread the roots into natural downward positions. Fill the hole and make sure that the crown is at surface level with no roots exposed and no soil on the crown. Firm with the sole of your shoe.

After planting, give the plants a good watering.

Annual care

When strawberries begin to flower, cover the soil with a layer of clean straw; work the straw under the leaves and flowers up to the crowns. This keeps the flowers and leaves off the soil and ensures clean fruit. It also increases the possibility of frost damage to flowers by stopping the warmth rising from the earth beneath, so delay 'strawing' as long as possible.

Strawberry plants are very hardy but their flowers are not. Frost-damaged flowers turn black in the centre and fail to form fruit. When the flowers are open (or about to open), cover the bed with one or two layers of fleece if frost is likely.

The fleece must be removed during the day to allow insects access for pollination. If your garden is subject to late spring frosts, avoid the early varieties of strawberry.

Pick fully ripe fruits, complete with a short length of stalk. To get the most from your strawberry bed, harvest every day during the fruiting period.

When fruiting has finished, clip off all the leaves to 10 cm (4 in) above the crowns. Collect the leaves, weeds and straw and dispose of them by burning them or taking them to the local tip.

During the summer runners appear. Root any that you need for forcing (see p 33) and clip the others off fairly close to the plant.

As the first fruits begin to ripen, cover the bed with a net; otherwise, the birds will peck the berries. A low wooden frame of tile laths is an ideal way to support a net. The net is hooked over slate nails left protruding slightly from the wood.

Grow your strawberries on a raised bed with a wooden surround. Cover the manured soil with a sheet of woven black plastic and staple it to the wood. Cut holes in the plastic and plant through them. This method removes the need for straw, as it keeps the fruit clean. In addition, the plastic controls weeds and helps to retain moisture.

Raspberries

A row of raspberry canes will produce good crops for 12 years or more. A row containing an early, a mid and a late season variety, plus an autumn-fruiting one, will give a continuous supply from June to November. Raspberries produce masses of fruit, half a kilo (1.1 lb) for each 30 cm (1 ft) of row every season.

Home-grown raspberries can also be enjoyed throughout the winter as they are easy to freeze. Spread the ripe fruit on a tray to freeze and, a few hours later, box them up.

All raspberries grow on canes. There are two types: summer fruiting and autumn fruiting. They need the same conditions but the pruning and staking are different.

Summer-fruiting raspberries produce fruit on the canes that grew the year before. In the summer the old canes produce fruit while a new crop of canes grows from soil level. After fruiting, the old canes change colour and die.

Autumn-fruiting raspberries grow new canes in early spring; these canes fruit in the autumn. Pruning autumn-fruiting raspberries is simple – cut all the canes off at ground level in February. Autumn-fruiting raspberry canes are not usually given any support.

Summer-fruiting raspberries

Raspberry canes can be planted any time between October and March; November is the best time. Buy new canes from a specialist fruit nursery: these will be subject to Government tests and certified healthy. Never accept gifts of canes from other gardeners, as they may have virus diseases.

Planting raspberry canes

Fix a 1.5 m (5 ft) post at either end of the row. Stretch two horizontal wires between the posts, one near to the top and the other half-way up. Tighten the top wire first; when tightening the bottom wire, take care not to slacken the top one.

Plant the canes 45 cm (18 in) apart. Make a large hole for each cane and spread the roots out carefully. Cover with 7.5 cm (3 in) of soil – do not plant any deeper than this. The canes may have been cut down by the grower. If not, cut the top off to three or four buds above the soil; this will leave about 30 cm (1 ft) of cane showing.

The following summer the short canes will grow flowering shoots. Pinch off the flowers. Hand weed as necessary; do not use a hoe. New canes will grow from the soil.

When the canes are tall enough, tie the strongest to the top and bottom wires. One cane every 10 cm (4 in) is ideal. After tying in the best canes, cut off weak and unwanted canes at soil level.

Water the canes in dry weather – this is very important during the first year.

Note Velcro ties are better than string – easier to tie and easier to undo the next year.

Good varieties:
'Glen Moy' – early; 'Malling Jewel' – mid season; 'Julia' – mid season; 'Leo' – late; 'Autumn Bliss' – autumn fruiting.

Annual care

March: Apply organic garden potash (or sulphate of potash) at the rate of 22 g per sq m (¾ oz/sq yd).

May: Mulch with well-rotted manure or garden compost. This will retain moisture, feed the plants and control weeds.

Summer: Harvest the fruits as they ripen. Pick only the fruit; leave the core on the plant. Remove weeds by hand as they appear.

Late summer: After the harvest, untie the old canes and cut them off just above soil level. Tie in the best of the new canes 10 cm (4 in) apart. Remove small and unwanted new canes by cutting them off at soil level.

Pruning summer-fruiting raspberries.

Autumn-fruiting raspberries

During April check the autumn-fruiting raspberries. If the new canes are becoming crowded, thin them out. There should be at least 10 cm (4 in) between one cane and the next.

Annual care

February: Cut old canes off at ground level.

March: Apply organic garden potash (or sulphate of potash) at the rate of 22 g per sq m (¾ oz/sq yd).

April: Thin out new canes to allow a minimum of 10 cm (4 in) between one cane and the next.

May: Mulch with rotted manure or garden compost.

Summer: Control weeds.

Autumn: Harvest the fruit as it ripens.

Blackcurrants

Blackcurrant bushes may be untidy but the fruit is superb. Blackcurrants are nutritious, have a strong flavour and are excellent in jams, jellies and pies. Blackcurrants freeze well, so a glut of fruit is not a problem.

A blackcurrant bush is a 'stool' with strong shoots arising from soil level. The stools need little attention apart from mulching, harvesting and pruning. Prune soon after the harvest is completed. The older the wood, the darker the bark. Because young wood carries the best fruit, your aim is to remove the old wood and leave the new. This is not too easy, as some of the new wood is growing on the old. Pruning cuts made near to ground level encourage new growth from the base of the plant. Growths in the middle of the stool need removing to keep the centre of the plant open.

Making it easier

An alternative pruning method is to cut off near to the ground all the stems that have fruited and leave the new stems to carry next year's fruit.

If you have two bushes (or more), cut one down to ground level in alternate years. One bush will fruit one year and the other the next. This method is wasteful of space but gives a good crop of top-quality berries.

Blackcurrants are vigorous plants that make a lot of growth and produce masses of fruit each year. To maintain this vigour, heavy dressings of well-rotted manure or garden compost are necessary. After pruning, apply a mulch around each plant; this also helps to control weeds.

The best variety for a small area is 'Ben Sarek'. The fruit is top quality and the bushes are small. If you buy 'Ben Sarek', reduce the planting distance to 90 cm (3 ft). A possible problem with this variety is that the crop is so heavy it may break the branches, but a piece of string tied round the bush gives enough support to prevent this. A good standard variety is 'Ben More', which is late flowering so there is less chance of frost damage.

November is the best time to plant new bushes although planting can continue until March. Buy two-year-old plants from a reputable source. Plant them at least 5 cm (2 in) deeper than the soil mark (assuming this is visible). Bushes need to be 1.5 m (5 ft) apart. After planting, cut off the stems, leaving 5 cm (2 in) above ground.

Every March give a top dressing of dried blood 90 g per sq m (3 oz/sq yd) followed by a deep mulch. If any weeds appear, remove them by hand. Harvest the fruit by picking individual berries or leave them a little longer and pick whole sprigs.

Red- and whitecurrants

The growth habit and pruning of redcurrants are very different from those of blackcurrants. Redcurrants are grown as a bush on a short stem or trained as cordons (single stems) against a wall or fence. Redcurrant bushes need treatment similar to that for gooseberry bushes (see below). The soil conditions are the same as for other soft fruit. Bare-root bushes can be planted at any time during the dormant period (from October to March), although late autumn is best. 'Redstart' is an excellent late variety and 'Laxton No. 1' is one of the best early varieties.

A whitecurrant is a variety of redcurrant, so needs exactly the same care.

Redcurrants are easy to prune, because fruit is borne on both new and old wood. Prune in the winter by cutting back the leaders (main branches) by half of the previous year's growth. Shorten the lateral growths (side branches) to leave them 5 cm (2 in) long. Remove any growths from the centre of the bush to maintain an open goblet shape.

A feed of organic garden potash, 56 g (2 oz) per bush, in the spring will increase the yield.

Gooseberry

A gooseberry is one of the few fruits that can be harvested before it ripens. It is usually grown on a bush that stands on a short leg. The gooseberry plant can also be trained into a cordon – or other shapes – against a wall.

Mildew is endemic on gooseberries and difficult to control. So it makes good sense to select a mildew-resistant variety such as 'Invicta'. 'Invicta' crops well and, unlike some other varieties, is fairly upright.

Plant gooseberry bushes during the winter, 1.5 m (5 ft) apart and the same depth as they were in the nursery – you can usually tell this from a soil mark on the stem.

Pruning – winter

A new gooseberry bush will have a number of leaders; cut these back half way. Always cut back to an upward-facing bud. Over the next few years create a goblet-shaped bush by removing growths from the centre and cutting back the leaders half way. Weak growths also need removing – cut them at the point of origin.

Pruning – summer

At the end of June cut all new lateral growths back to leave five leaves on each.

Other care

Apply an annual mulch to feed the plants and control the weeds. In May, examine the bushes regularly for gooseberry sawfly. These small caterpillars start eating the leaves at the base of the plant and quickly defoliate it. Kill any caterpillars you find and spray the plants with BT (see p 120).

Apples

Apples are an interesting and rewarding crop to grow. The size and shape of tree can be adapted to suit your garden and to keep all parts within easy reach for pruning and other operations.

A single apple tree will not fruit unless there is a different variety nearby, flowering at the same time, to cross-pollinate. A few varieties need two pollinators. 'Family' trees have three compatible varieties growing on a single stem. Such trees can be successful but require very careful pruning. If you have enough space, it is better to grow two or three trees of different varieties.

Almost all apple trees are two different kinds of tree joined, just above soil level, by budding or grafting. The roots (root stock) control the size and vigour of the tree whilst the top determines the type of fruit. This combination allows apples to be grown on trees of various sizes from small 'step-overs' to large standards. Cordons, espaliers, single column, spindles, half standards and several other shapes are possible. The bush tree is the easiest shape to prune and possibly the most productive.

When you buy apple trees, two things are extremely important:

- The trees are growing on the correct root stock for your requirements.

- The selected varieties will cross-pollinate satisfactorily.

Any reputable fruit nursery will be able to supply this information.

The branches of this tree were tied into a horizontal position during its first years of growth

Growing bush apple trees

For information on tree planting and staking, see pages 45 and 46.

Container-grown apple trees can be planted at any time of the year. If you are going to buy a container-grown tree, reject any with roots protruding from the container. There is a danger with container-grown trees that the roots will fail to grow into the surrounding soil. When you are planting the tree, tease out its roots from the outside of the root ball. Bare-root trees often do better than container-grown ones for this reason. Whatever type you buy, it will need shaping.

The final shape of a tree depends upon its treatment during the first three years. Begin to shape your trees immediately after planting. You should aim for a goblet shape with an empty centre. Horizontal branches grow with less vigour and produce more fruit than vertical ones. A new apple tree should arrive either as a 'maiden', consisting of a single vertical stalk, or a 'feathered maiden', which has several long growths called feathers.

To shape a maiden tree into a bush:

- Cut off the top, just above a bud, 1 metre (3 ft 3 in) from the ground. (*Omit this first step for a feathered maiden.*)

- The following year several of the buds will develop into shoots.

- Remove any shoots that are less than 60 cm (2 ft) from the ground.

- Select four or five of the others and, with extreme care (don't break them off!), tie them into a near-horizontal position with string pegged into the ground (these branches will be the main framework of the tree).

- In the autumn remove the strings.

- In the winter shorten each branch by about half its length, cutting to a downward-facing bud.

- The following year tie down the new wood growing from the ends of the branches, to maintain horizontal growth.

Cordons are pruned in summer. Towards the end of July cut back any new growth 25 cm (10 in) long or longer, to leave three buds. Wait until mid-September and treat the smaller growths in the same way.

Pruning an established bush apple tree

Unlike most other shapes, an established bush apple need not be pruned in the summer. It is pruned in winter to maintain its shape and to regulate growth. Pruning also improves cropping. If last season's growth is left unpruned, two or three buds on the ends develop and the rest remain dormant. This means a lot of bare, unproductive wood. To prevent this, shorten the laterals by cutting them back to leave four or five buds. At this time it is possible to distinguish between the fruit buds and other buds, because fruit buds are fatter. The leaders (growths at the ends of the branches) should not be cut back nearly as hard and, after a few years, are better left unpruned.

Pruning guide (winter)

- Remove any dead or diseased wood.
- Cut out any branch that is crossing the centre of the tree.
- If two branches are rubbing together, remove one.
- Cut back all laterals to five buds.
- Leave the leaders unpruned.

If you have to prune a neglected tree, you will need a saw to remove some of the branches. Spread the pruning over two or more years, so that no more than 10 per cent of the wood is cut off in any one year.

An annual mulch of organic matter feeds the tree and keeps the soil in good condition. It also controls grass and other weeds that would otherwise compete with the tree.

Thinning the fruit

In June (or possibly early July) several of the fruitlets drop off. This is quite normal and is known as the 'June drop'. After the 'June drop' some varieties are still loaded with fruits. If left, they will be small and of poor quality. In addition, the tree will be put under strain and may not fruit the following year. Where the apples are in tight clusters, remove all but one from each cluster. Elsewhere reduce pairs of apples to singles.

Harvesting

The usual test for ripeness is to give an apple a gentle lift and twist. If the apple breaks off easily, it is ready for harvest. Another test is to cut open an apple and check the colour of the pips: if they are brown, the apples are ready to be harvested. The wasps and birds are also indicators that your apples are beginning to ripen. If you notice that an apple is being eaten by wasps, do not pick it, as the wasps will only start on another apple. A wasp trap may prevent further damage. (A wasp trap consists of a jam jar half filled with sugar water and covered by a paper lid with a hole in the centre for wasps to get in.) Apples must be treated with the same care as eggs, especially if they are to be stored.

You can store sound fruits of later varieties by wrapping them individually in a page from a magazine and laying them in a single layer of a slatted tray. They need a cool, frost-free place, and different varieties should be stored in separate trays.

An alternative method is to store the apples in small numbers in perforated plastic bags. Whatever method you use, cool conditions are essential and you must regularly check for and remove any blemished fruit. Blemished apples can be peeled, sliced, blanched and frozen for later use in pies and apple sauce.

Grease bands wrapped round the trunk in late autumn are often recommended to control winter moth. I never use these, because winter moth caterpillars are excellent food for nestling birds. A garden with plenty of birds will not have significant winter moth damage. (See pages 120 and 121 for codling moth control to keep your apples grub-free.)

Pears

Pears are grown in a similar way to apples. Pear blossom is earlier than apple blossom and therefore more likely to be affected by late frost.

Stone fruit

The more exotic stone fruits such as peaches are best left to the enthusiasts. If you have enough space to accommodate half-standard trees, plums and damsons are the best choice. If you have a south- or south-west-facing wall that could accommodate a fan-shaped tree, a Victoria plum would be ideal. Although the best-flavoured fruit is obtained by growing against a warm wall, plums do very well in the open.

Plums and damsons are unsuitable for growing as small, shaped plants. The smallest plum trees available are worked on 'Pixi' root stock, which grows to a height of 2.5 metres – a little over 8 feet. These need a space 3 m (10 ft) wide. Trees on other root stocks are larger and need more space.

Many plum varieties are self-sterile and need a different variety nearby that flowers at the same time. Even plums advertised as 'self-fertile' (eg Victoria) set a better crop when pollinated by a different variety. In some years crops are so heavy that the branches need propping to prevent them from breaking.

Pruning

Stone fruit is subject to a fungus disease called 'silver leaf' that may kill the tree. To prevent the disease, prune when the tree is in full leaf; the wounds will then be sealed naturally. The best time is immediately after harvest. In practice, very little pruning is necessary. Leave the trees to 'do their own thing' until they are fruiting. After that, pruning consists of removing crossing branches and growths crowding the centre of the tree. Of course, cut out any dead or diseased wood.

Thinning

Plums often set large quantities of fruit. If you leave them all to develop, they will be small and rather dry. Thin them out to leave no more than one fruit per 5 cm (2 in) of stem. Although there will be fewer fruits, those that remain will be large and juicy.

Harvesting

Fruit left on the tree until it is fully ripe has the best flavour. Take the ripe fruits and leave the rest to ripen. This gives a harvest period of between two and three weeks. Fruit intended for jam making can be harvested before it is quite ripe.

Grubs in plums

A pheromone trap, similar to the one described on page 120 and fitted with the correct pheromone, is very effective in controlling plum moth. The other main pest problem is the plum leaf-curling aphid – for control methods see page 119.

Chapter 7

Food You Can Trust

Retirement will allow you time to enjoy growing and eating some home-produced food. This really does taste better because of its freshness and freedom from chemical residues. If you have space for a vegetable plot, you can be almost self-sufficient in vegetables. Even if your garden is small, you can produce the occasional gourmet delight from the patio, greenhouse or the odd fruit tree. You can also have your own continuous supply of herbs, either fresh or home frozen.

Raised beds

Raised beds are the ideal way to grow vegetables. Note that the rows run across the width of the bed and not down its length. Details of raised beds are given on pages 8 and 9.

Fertilisers

In order to grow, plants need carbon from the air, hydrogen and oxygen from water and 14 or so other elements from the soil. If any element is in short supply, your plants will grow more slowly. The aim of using fertilisers is to make good any shortfall. The three elements most likely to be in short supply are nitrogen, phosphorus and potassium. In gardening these are normally referred to as nitrate, phosphate and potash – N:P:K – in that order. A fertiliser that contains 15 per cent nitrate, 5 per cent phosphate and 10 per cent potash will have 15:5:10 printed on the container.

Soil that has an annual dressing of organic matter at the rate of 5 kg per sq m (10 lb/sq yd) will contain sufficient phosphate and potash for maximum yields. Where it is not possible to add those quantities of manure, spread the following over the surface in early spring and lightly rake in:

- 70 g per sq m (2 oz/sq yd) rock phosphate or superphosphate.

- 35 g per sq m (1 oz/sq yd) of organic garden potash or sulphate of potash.

Nitrogen is the element that is most often in short supply. A small amount of nitrate fertiliser, applied at the correct time, will have a large effect on yield. Nitrate can be applied organically as dried blood or as a chemical fertiliser. Nitro chalk or sulphate of ammonia are probably the best choices.

Too much nitrate is harmful, as it produces weak growth, delays maturity and can cause environmental damage. Nitrogen encourages leaf growth and is best applied to the soil around plants immediately before a period of active growth. When used in this way, the chemical will be taken up by the plant and not leached away with the drainage water.

You may find that a compound fertiliser – one that contains nitrate, phosphate and potash – is the most convenient to use. There is an organic one 6:6:6 and a chemical one, Growmore, that is 7:7:7. If you use a compound fertiliser, there is no need to add phosphate and potash separately.

Most soils tend to become acid over time. For maximum yields the acid measurement (pH) needs to be between 6.0 and 7.0. Use a garden centre testing kit every three years and add lime if necessary. The kit gives details of the amounts needed. The best time to lime is after a crop has been removed. Spread ground limestone over the surface and lightly rake it into the top 5 cm (2 in). Do not manure at the same time; manuring should be delayed for a few weeks. Liming is a very dusty job, so choose a still day and wear a mask and eye protection.

Planting

Module-raised lettuce and beetroot plants ready for planting outside.

Almost all vegetables can be grown by sowing directly into the soil. However, there are many advantages in raising plants elsewhere and transplanting them when they are established.

The advantages of using plants instead of direct-sown seeds are:

- The crop is in the ground for less time.
- Earlier crops.
- Longer cropping period.
- Less dependent on the weather.
- Easier pest control.
- Better control of plant populations.
- Use fewer seeds.
- Easier weed control.
- Additional crop (sometimes).

The disadvantages of using plants are:

- You need to raise the plants elsewhere or buy them.
- Additional cost of propagation equipment.

There are very few crops that do not benefit from transplanting; these include parsnips, turnips and carrots. Plants are best raised in Rootrainers: 'Fleet's for beans, brassicas and sweetcorn; 'Sherwood's for others. Transplant into beds before the roots become tightly packed.

Equipment

If you use raised beds, you will need surprisingly little equipment. All I use is a garden rake, a soil scoop, an onion hoe, a watering can, a fork, a wheelbarrow, an assortment of garden canes, a ball of string and my pocket knife. There is one additional item that I consider essential – a staple gun.

Making it easier

A staple gun is a quick and easy method of fixing all types of plastic sheeting and nets.

A soil scoop digs holes faster and more easily than a trowel.

In order to grow good organic vegetables you will need some means of raising plants. An electric propagator in a cold greenhouse is ideal. Otherwise a warm windowsill, with good light and little direct sun, can be used for germination and a cold frame for growing on. (See pages 20–23 for methods of raising plants.)

Sowing

Vegetables such as parsnips, radishes, carrots and turnips are sown directly into the soil.

Having raked the soil to a fine tilth, draw straight, parallel drills the correct width apart.

Soak the bottom of the drills from the spout of a watering can.

Sow the seeds very thinly and cover with a multipurpose compost.

After germination, hoe between the rows to remove seedling weeds. Thin the seedlings to leave singles half the final distance apart. When the plants are growing well, thin a second time to the correct distance. Water in very dry weather.

Crop rotation

Crop rotation means that a single bed will grow a different crop each year for either three or four years. This has the effect of reducing disease, increasing yields, controlling weeds and keeping the soil in good heart. The simplest system, and the most effective for a small area, is a three-year rotation (for details, see p 11).

Making it easier

The easiest way to grow vegetables is to plant good plants in a raised bed. You do not have to raise these plants yourself, because several of the well-known seed companies supply vegetable plants by post. The plants are all proven varieties and arrive at the correct planting time. An added advantage is that the plants are pest- and disease-free.

Plants purchased by post have been raised in ideal conditions and need a little extra care. Given the right conditions they romp away to maturity. Plant them as soon as they arrive and cover them with a layer of fleece. With crops such as cabbage the fleece can remain in place until maturity – provided there is enough slack to allow for growth.

Sadly, many of the vegetable plants I see in garden centres have been too long on display and are past their best. Never buy inferior plants.

Uncommon vegetables

It can be fun to grow uncommon vegetables but there is usually a good reason why they are uncommon. The common vegetables are popular because they are easy and rewarding to grow. If your garden has limited space, it is probably better to experiment with different varieties of the common vegetables than use space for the less common ones.

Winged peas are said to have an asparagus flavour. They are attractive plants but the pods must be harvested when very small; this is a slow process and the flavour is disappointing.

For some reason, which I do not understand, catalogues often describe small varieties as 'suitable for small gardens'. Taller varieties make better use of available space and produce high yields in small gardens as well as in large ones.

Some differences between beetroot varieties are easily seen. There are also differences that cannot be seen – these include earliness, taste, resistance to 'bolting' and disease.

Common vegetables, in alphabetical order

The timings given below are for the Midlands. In other areas the operations may be later or earlier, depending on your local conditions and climate. The planting dates of some vegetables depend on the date of the last frost. If you live in a frost hollow, as I do, your last frost may be several days later than higher gardens a few hundred yards away. Gardens in large cities are warmer than those in the surrounding countryside; as a result, they have more frost-free days.

Beetroot

Beetroots are easy to grow, either sown direct into the soil or germinated in modules and transplanted in clumps of three to five. If young plants are subjected to cold conditions, they will 'bolt' (run to seed instead of forming a beetroot). It is better to delay sowing by two weeks or so rather than have a crop that bolts. Beetroot can also be grown in containers and under cloches. Beetroot 'seeds' are clusters of several seeds and will produce a few plants per cluster. Monogerm seeds produce one plant per seed. A little cooking salt, sprinkled either side of a row soon after germination, is beneficial. Water beetroot in dry weather, but not too much or the plants will produce leaves rather than roots.

Beetroot is a maritime plant that benefits from a small amount of salt. Dissolve two tablespoons of salt in a full can and water along the row.

Immediately after harvest, you should twist off the tops (never cut them off).

March: Sow 'Boltardy' in sectioned trays (two seeds per section) of multipurpose compost. Germinate in a warm room (or propagator) and then transfer to the greenhouse or cold frame.
April: Plant clumps of five seedlings 15 cm (6 in) apart in a greenhouse bed or under cloches that have been in place for two weeks. When the roots are large enough, harvest by rotating the larger ones between finger and thumb, leaving the others to grow.
May: Sow an early variety outdoors to provide succession. Sow a main-crop variety outdoors and thin out to 10 cm (4 in) apart to produce larger beetroots for chutney or use as a vegetable.
June: Make a final sowing of an early variety for succession.

Broad beans

Broad bean plants in Rootrainers ready for transplanting.

Broad beans are a cold weather crop and sowings made after the end of April are unlikely to produce a worthwhile harvest. Some white-seeded varieties are suitable for autumn sowing and will survive the winter in most parts of the country – not recommended on heavy soils, though. Green-seeded varieties have a better flavour; these can only be sown in the spring.

An aphid known as 'blackfly' is a serious pest of broad beans. The best method of control is to grow an early crop by raising the plants inside and then transplanting them. Blackflies feed on the growing tip and later move down to the flower buds. Removing the top of a plant as soon as the aphids arrive gives good control. Ants climbing the plants indicate the presence of blackfly – and you can see ants more easily than small numbers of blackfly!

Tall varieties of broad beans need some support. One good method is to fix a horizontal net 45 cm (18 in) above the crop for it to grow through. The net can be raised later to accommodate tall varieties. Beans in rows can be supported with two horizontal strings each side of the row, tied to end stakes. Additional support can be obtained by joining the long strings on either side of the row with short lengths of string.

Harvest your broad beans when the pods are full and the scars on the seeds are green. If the scar has become black, the beans will be tough.

February: Sow seeds individually 5 cm (2 in) deep in 7.5 cm (3 in) pots or deep Rootrainers. Germinate in a warm room or propagator.
March: As soon as the seedlings emerge, move them to a cold greenhouse or cold frame.
April: Warm the soil for two weeks with plastic or cloches. Then plant out in double rows, 25 cm (9 in) apart, with 25 cm (9 in) between the plants and 45 cm (18 in) between each double row. Cover with fleece for two weeks.
May: Arrange supports. Control weeds.
June: Harvest the pods soon after they have filled.
July: When harvesting is complete, cut the plants off at ground level and sow lettuce, endive and Chinese cabbage. (Leave the roots in the earth because they contain valuable plant food.)

Brussels sprouts

Brussels sprouts are very hardy and high yielding. You can achieve a continuous supply of fresh sprouts throughout the winter by growing two varieties. Sprouts can be harvested from September to March. The flower buds, produced in April, make a delicious vegetable.

Brussels sprouts need a lot of space – 90 cm (35 in) between the plants. They also need a firm soil and strong stakes.

99

Good varieties:
'Peer Gynt' for an early crop and 'Trafalgar' for a late one.

Open buttons, like the one on the right, are the result of growing in loose soil.

March/early April: Germinate the seeds in a propagator; prick out the seedlings into individual pots or deep Rootrainers.
May: Harden off and transplant outside, 90 cm (35 in) apart. Water the plants until they are established.
June: Apply Nitro chalk or dried blood, 50 g per sq m (2 oz/sq yd).
July: Repeat the dressing of fertiliser.
Summer: Control aphids and caterpillars (see Chapter 8 for pest control).
August: Stake each plant with a strong garden cane and two string ties.
Autumn/winter: Harvest sprouts regularly. Remove all leaves as they yellow and die.
April: Harvest young shoots. Pull up and dispose of old plants.

Cabbage

Given sufficient space, it is possible to have cabbages all the year round. If you don't have much space, you can choose between spring, summer and winter crops. The best choice is probably spring, as fresh vegetables are less plentiful in May/June. Traditional spring cabbages are not easy, because the sowing date is critical and weather patterns are changing. Crops may die in winter or bolt in spring. I recommend substituting spring cabbage with early summer types sown in February.

Cabbages are produced by raising plants and transplanting. The size of cabbage depends on both variety and spacing. A well-manured soil will produce a crop of cabbage without your needing to use fertiliser. Yields are considerably increased if you add nitrogen fertiliser at the appropriate times. The endemic disease, clubroot, is less active in neutral soil (pH around 7.0). Transplants with good root balls attached are less affected by clubroot than are bare-root transplants.

An insect-proof cage made from wooden tile laths and enviromesh.

A very effective way to control caterpillars, aphids and whitefly on cabbages is to grow them under enviromesh. If it is not possible to plant out in an enviromesh 'cage', cover the plants with fleece immediately after transplanting them, to prevent damage by cabbage root fly.

Good varieties:
Spring: 'Hispi' (pointed); summer: 'Quickstep'; winter: 'January King' and 'Tundra'.

After harvesting a cabbage, if you leave the stalk in the ground a second crop of small cabbages often develops.

'Spring' cabbage

February: Make two sowings of 'Hispi', four weeks apart, and germinate them in a propagator. Prick out into individual pots or Rootrainers.

April: Plant out in a greenhouse bed or under cloches that have been in position for at least two weeks. Spacing: 20 × 20 cm (8 × 8 in) (plant only the number of plants you will need, as 'Hispi' remains in harvesting condition for only a week; after that time, the 'heart' splits open).

May/June: Harvest as soon as ready.

Summer cabbage

March: Sow in pots and germinate in a propagator. Prick out into individual pots or Rootrainers. Grow on in a cold greenhouse or cold frame.

May: Transplant into firm soil 35 × 35 cm (14 × 14 in) apart and water until established.

June: Apply Nitro chalk or dried blood, 50 g per sq m (2 oz/sq yd).

July to October: In dry weather give a good soaking two weeks before harvesting. Harvest as required. After harvesting, cut a cross on the top of the stem for a second crop.

Winter cabbage

May: Sow seeds and raise plants as for summer cabbage.

June: Transplant into firm soil 50 × 50 cm (20 × 20 in) apart. Water until established.

Summer: Water only during very dry weather. Control weeds by hand or very shallow hoeing.

Winter: Harvest as required. Remove dead leaves.

Calabrese (broccoli)

This crop of side shoots grew after the main head had been harvested. Regular harvesting may result in a third and possibly a fourth crop

The best varieties of calabrese crop over a long period. After the main head is cut, side shoots grow, which carry smaller heads. Surplus calabrese can be blanched and frozen.

Home-grown calabrese should be inspected very carefully for caterpillars or slugs concealed in the heads.

Good varieties:
'Mercedes' and 'Corvet' (for cold districts).

April: Sow and raise plants as for cabbage.
May: Plant out 45 cm (18 in) apart and protect with fleece. Provided you leave enough slack to allow for growth, the fleece can be left on until harvest.
Summer: Control weeds; water in dry weather. Harvest regularly before the flower buds begin to open.

Carrot

Carrot fly is easily controlled by surrounding the bed with a fleece barrier. There is no need to cover the top, because the fly keeps near to the ground when searching for a place to lay her eggs.

The structure of the soil is all-important for growing carrots. Soil needs to be friable to allow easy root penetration; otherwise, the roots become fanged. If your soil is unsuitable, grow carrots in containers (see p 78).

Grow small, stump-rooted, quick-maturing carrots for an early crop. Larger varieties are grown as a main crop. 'Early' varieties can also be sown towards the end of summer to produce a late crop.

Good varieties:
'Amsterdam Forcing' (early) and 'Autumn King' (main crop).

March: Prepare a fine tilth. Sow seeds, of an early variety, very thinly in rows 15 cm (6 in) apart. Cover the seeds with a thin layer of multipurpose compost.
April: Erect a carrot fly barrier.
May: Sow a main-crop variety in a similar way.
June: Water with care in dry weather – apply water to the soil and not the foliage. Harvest from the March sowing by pulling the largest roots and leaving the others to grow. Remove the tops immediately after harvesting the carrots. Thin the main-crop variety to 5 cm (2 in) apart.
December: Cover the main crop with straw (or other protective material) to protect from frost. This is better than lifting and storing. Harvest as required.

Cauliflower

Summer cauliflowers are annuals, producing curds in the year they are sown. Winter cauliflowers are biennials and require a period of cold before they develop curds. They are sown one year and harvested the next. The plants are hardy but the curds are not. Winter cauliflowers are unlikely to succeed in cold districts, because frost is likely during curd formation.

Cauliflowers need to make rapid and uninterrupted growth; otherwise, the curds will be small. To achieve good growth the soil must be well manured to supply both water and nutrients. In addition, the soil must provide a firm anchorage. To firm the soil, prepare it well in advance and leave it to consolidate. Treading the soil before planting may do more harm than good.

Good varieties:
Summer cauliflower: 'Dok Elgon' and 'All the Year Round'; winter cauliflower: 'Arcade' (mid-March) and 'Walcheren Armado' (mid-April).

Summer cauliflower

Previous autumn: Prepare the cauliflower bed.
March: Sow in pots, germinate in a propagator, and prick out into individual pots or Rootrainers filled with multipurpose compost.
April: Grow on in a cold greenhouse or cold frame.
May: Harden off and plant out 60 cm (2 ft) apart. A closer spacing will give smaller curds, but more of them – minimum distance 50 cm (20 in). Cover with fleece to protect from insect pests.
Summer: Water as required; control weeds. Harvest as soon as ready. Cauliflowers often mature all at the same time. Some succession can be obtained by transplanting half the plants one week and the rest a week later. After harvesting, a cauliflower continues to develop and may spoil. Wrapping a freshly harvested cauliflower in cling film and placing it in a refrigerator will prevent further development.

Winter cauliflower

May: Raise plants in a cold frame or cold greenhouse.
July: Transplant 76 cm (30 in) apart and water in.
Summer: Control weeds, and water if necessary. Protect from caterpillars by covering with fleece or spraying with BT (see p 120).
February: Top dress with dried blood or Nitro chalk.
March/April: Inspect regularly and harvest as soon as ready.

Chinese cabbage

Pak choi – one of the many Chinese vegetables that are easy to grow in this part of the world.

Chinese cabbage is very hardy. There are several different types. They can be cooked like cabbage or used in stir-fry. Chinese cabbage is often recommended to be used in green salad but I find that most types are too tough to be eaten raw.

Given good light, and some protection from wind, Chinese cabbage is easy to grow. Delay sowing until after the first of July – this makes it an ideal catch crop to follow early potatoes or broad beans. Chinese cabbage is subject to the same pests as cabbages, especially cabbage root fly.

Good varieties:
'Wong Bok' (large hearts) and 'Tah Tsai' (non-hearting).

July: Sow seeds direct into the soil in rows 40 cm (16 in) apart.
August: Thin seedlings to 40 cm (16 in) apart. Water in dry weather and mulch.
September onwards: Harvest.

Note If large varieties fail to heart, tie the tops loosely together with raffia.

April: Sow seeds singly in 12 cm (5 in) pots of multipurpose compost. Germinate on the greenhouse bench or a windowsill. Prepare a bed by mixing large quantities of organic matter with the soil from a square metre to produce a mound.
May: Harden off plants at the end of the month.
June: Plant one plant per mound.
July: For courgettes, remove male flowers (they don't have a small courgette on the flower stalk) and harvest courgettes regularly. For marrows, pollinate by removing a male flower, pulling off the petals and placing it inside a female.
Summer: Continue to harvest courgettes; protect developing marrows by slipping a board underneath.

Courgettes (and marrows)

Courgettes will give you a high-yielding crop provided you harvest it regularly. Unharvested courgettes quickly turn into marrows.

Courgettes need a free-draining soil and a constant supply of water. A single plant will usually supply the needs of a small family. If you grow two or more plants, they need to be a metre (39 in) apart. Bush varieties are easier to manage, because trailing varieties need lots of space.

Good varieties:
'Zucchini' for courgettes and 'Badger Cross' for marrows.

French beans

This quick-maturing half-hardy annual is a 'must' for any household. Pencil-podded types freeze more successfully than runner beans. There are two forms: bush and climbing. They grow best in a moist, warm soil and do exceptionally well in containers of multipurpose compost.

Good varieties:
'Ferrari' (bush, pencil podded) and 'Algarve' (climbing, flat podded).

After planting courgettes, sink a pot alongside the plant. The water you pour into the pot will supply the roots instead of running off the mound.

May: Wait until the soil is at least 10°C (50°F) and sow seeds, 5 cm (2 in) deep, directly in the soil, 15 cm (6 in) apart. Sow two seeds per 'station'.
June: Remove the weakest seedling from each pair by nipping it off at ground level. Control weeds.
July: Top dress with dried blood, 30 g per sq m (1 oz/sq yd). Water when the flowers begin to open. If there is little rain, apply 22 litres per sq m (4 gal/sq yd) of water every week. Harvest regularly.
August/September: Continue to water in dry weather. If water is in short supply, give one good watering and then mulch. Harvest at least twice a week, taking all the crop that is ready each time.

plant in pots in November and grow in a cold greenhouse or cold frame until early March and then transplant outside. Harvest in July when the tops begin to yellow. Dry them and hang in 'ropes'.

Good variety:
'Silverskin'.

November or February: Plant individual cloves, with the tips just under the surface, 15 cm (6 in) apart in rows 30 cm (12 in) apart.
March to June: Keep weed-free by hand or shallow hoeing.
July: Lift with a fork, dry thoroughly, tie into ropes and store.

Garlic

Breaking a garlic bulb into cloves ready for planting.

Garlic is very easy to grow and there are almost no pest or disease problems. In order for a garlic plant to form a bulb, it must be subject to several weeks of cold weather. On light soils in the south, garlic can be planted in November. In other areas, and on heavy soils, plant in February. An alternative is to

Note A garlic clove planted at the base of a rose is said to deter greenfly. A garlic clove planted at the base of a tomato will improve the flavour of the tomatoes.

Leeks

Leeks are a very winter-hardy, reliable crop that will grow in most soils. For large crops, you must have a well-manured soil with a pH around 7.0.

*After placing a leek plant in its planting hole, fill the hole with water – do **not** fill with soil.*

The traditional way to get a good length of blanched stem is to 'earth up' the leeks with soil. Whenever I have done this, soil particles get down the leaves and spoil parts of the leek. A much easier method is to use scrap builders' materials such as plastic downpipes.

As soon as the leeks are large enough, place a piece of plastic pipe over each one to increase the extent of blanched stem.

Old clay drainpipes may also be used to blanch leeks.

Good varieties:
'King Richard' (early) and 'Laura' (late).

Autumn: Prepare the soil by adding lots of manure or compost.
March: Sow an early variety very thinly in pots in a greenhouse or on windowsill. Grow on in good light.
May: Sow seeds of a late variety in the same way.
June: Harden off the first sowing. Make holes with the handle of a trowel, 7.5 cm (3 in) deep and 15 cm (6 in) apart, along rows 30 cm (12 in) apart. Lower one seedling into each hole and fill the hole with water.
July: Plant the late variety in a similar way but allow 20 cm (8 in) between the plants. Control weeds.
August: Cover the early variety with lengths of rainwater downpipes.
September onwards: Remove any flower buds that appear. Harvest by digging up the entire plant. Transfer the blanching pipe to another leek.

Notes
1 Many gardeners trim the roots and leaves of leek plants as they transplant. I see no value in this practice.
2 You can grow small leeks by putting three or four plants into one planting hole.

Lettuce

Lettuce is by far the most popular salad crop, and for very good reasons. The aim is to have a continuous supply without large gluts. The best way for you to achieve this is to sow several varieties at the same time and repeat five weeks later. Choose varieties with care – summer varieties will fail in winter.

Any free-draining, moisture-retentive soil will produce a crop of lettuce. Watering improves both the size and quality of lettuce. Water twice a week in dry weather. A dressing of dried blood or Nitro chalk at the rate of 30 g per sq m (1 oz/sq yd) before planting is beneficial. Early in the season a

Different varieties have different development times. By sowing several at the same time, you will extend the cropping period.

cover of fleece or wire mesh is essential to prevent sparrows from pecking the leaves. Summer transplants may run to seed before forming a heart – sowing straight into the soil and thinning out as soon as the seedlings are large enough to handle helps to prevent this.

There are four main types of lettuce:

- *Butterhead* – hearted lettuce with soft leaves.
- *Crisphead* – hearted with crisp leaves.
- *Cos* – slow-maturing plants with upright elongated hearts.
- *Loose leaf* – a rosette of leaves that do not heart.

Good varieties:
'Little Gem' (cos), 'Tom Thumb' (butterhead), 'Saladin' (crisp head), 'Lollo Rossa' (loose leaf), 'Kellys' (crisp head, greenhouse winter lettuce).

February: Sow several varieties in pots in a greenhouse or on a windowsill. Prick out into individual pots or Rootrainers.
April: Harden off and transplant under cloches or fleece.
April to July: Sow in open ground; make a new sowing when you thin out the previous sowing. Hand weed and thin out to 20 cm (8 in) apart – larger distances for the bigger varieties, according to the instructions on the packet.
All summer: Harvest as soon as the hearts are firm by cutting off at ground level, or take individual leaves from loose leaf varieties – it is often better to cut the whole plant.
November: Sow the variety 'Kellys' in the greenhouse and grow on in a soil bed. Growth throughout the winter is very slow; the plants form good hearts in late April – if they have not been affected by fungus diseases.

Lettuce can be planted in any spare piece of ground. Here use is being made of the path between two rows of peas. The lettuce will be harvested before the path is required for pea picking.

Onions

Except for potatoes, onions are the most important culinary vegetable. The onion plant is a biennial that is harvested half way through its life cycle. Onions are easy to grow from seed and even easier to grow from sets (small juvenile onions that grow into larger ones).

In common with almost all other vegetables, onions need to be grown in full sun in a fertile, well-drained soil with a pH of around 6.5. Onion leaves are easily damaged by wind; if your site is windy, a wind break (see p 11) will improve the yield. Onions need more weeding than most crops, as the leaves cast very little shade (which inhibits weeds).

> **Good varieties:**
> Sets: 'Stuttgart Giant'; seeds: 'Hygro', 'Ailsa Craig' and 'Kelsae' (large).

Large crops of small onions can be obtained by sowing five seeds in each cell of a Rootrainer. The resulting plants are planted in clumps 20 cm (8 in) apart.

Growing from seed

January: For extra-large onions, sow 'Kelsa' in multipurpose compost and germinate in a propagator.
February: Prick out into individual 7.5 cm (3 in) pots. Grow on in a greenhouse, if possible giving supplementary lighting.
April: Plant out in a well-prepared bed. Erect a wind break of fleece.
May to September: As for sets (below).

Growing from sets

March/early April: Plant onion sets firmly under the soil with the tips just showing. Space the sets 5 cm (2 in) apart along rows that are 25 cm (10 in) apart. Cover with fleece to prevent sparrows pulling them up.
May: Water with seaweed extract and top dress with dried blood or Nitro chalk at the rate of 30 g per sq m (1 oz/sq yd).
May to July: Hand weed as necessary (don't hoe, because very fine roots are near the surface). Remove the flower bud from any that bolt. Water in very dry weather, but do not water after mid-July.
August: Ease plants up with a fork, and harvest two weeks later. Dry them off the in the sun. Onions keep better if they are harvested before the end of August.
September: Tie them into ropes and hang them in a cold, frost-free place.

Easing onions with a fork in mid-August to encourage the tops to fall (never bend the tops over by hand).

The dried leaves of onions are strong enough to attach the bulbs to a rope.

A small area of fresh parsley is extremely useful – especially if it is near the kitchen door.

The seeds will germinate in two to three weeks. Grow on in good light, harden off and plant out; separate the plants with care to keep as much compost on the roots as possible.

When harvesting parsley, never strip a plant of all its leaves – leave a few large ones on each plant. These will feed the root and speed up regrowth. Surplus leaves can be chopped and frozen.

Sow in March for a summer crop and again in July for a later crop. Protect with cloches in early winter.

> Good varieties:
> 'Darki' (curled leaves) and 'French' (plain leaves – stronger flavour).

Salad onions

Salad or spring onions grow very slowly. They can be sown, fairly thickly, in bands across a weed-free raised bed. Harvest by pulling the larger ones, leaving the smaller ones to grow. Unused spring onions form small bulbs that can be used for cooking.

Better spring onions are grown in a cold greenhouse, or on the patio in containers of multipurpose compost. The method to use is exactly the same as for carrots (see p 78).

Parsley

Parsley can be difficult to germinate but the following method usually succeeds. Fill a 12.5 cm (5 in) pot with multipurpose compost and water it. Make seven small holes in the compost 1 cm (0.5 in) deep. Drop one parsley seed into the bottom of each hole. Do not cover the seeds (light assists germination). Place the pot in a heated propagator or on the windowsill of a warm room.

Peas

Home-grown peas are much better flavoured than any from the supermarket – fresh or frozen.

An open site with plenty of sunshine and little wind is ideal. Peas will grow in any well-managed soil provided it is not too acid (pH less than 6). Crop succession is difficult, because later sowings often catch up with earlier ones. Sowing two or three varieties at the same time is a good way to achieve succession. Late sowings often fail to produce a satisfactory crop because there is less sunshine in the autumn. Home-grown peas freeze extremely well, reducing the importance of succession.

A common cause of failure is sowing peas in cold soil – the soil needs to be 10°C (50°F) or warmer; otherwise the seeds may rot. Your earliest crops will be obtained by raising pea plants in Rootrainers and transplanting. This also solves the problem of mice digging up the germinating seeds!

Early in the season, sparrows peck the young shoots; a layer of fleece prevents this (but not the ravages of slugs). Tall varieties must be staked with a net or twiggy sticks. Short varieties can be grown without stakes but they crop better with some support.

Making it easier

The variety 'Markarna' has masses of tendrils and the plants support each other. A few garden canes, with strings tied between, will provide all the support needed.

In order to get a good yield, peas must be correctly spaced. A triple row, 11 cm (4 in) apart with the seeds placed 11 cm (4 in) apart along the row, is best. If you are going to grow more than one row, allow 60 cm (2 ft) between the rows.

Harvest the peas as soon as the pods have filled. Take care during the first picking not to disturb the plants. Use two hands: support the plant with one hand and pull off the pod with the other. It is easier to find and harvest the pods if you pull the plants up during the final picking.

> **Good varieties:**
> Early: 'Beagle'; main crop: 'Hurst Greenshaft'; mangetout: 'Carouby de Mausanne'.

> *April:* Sow an early variety direct into the soil or transplant Rootrainer-grown plants.
> *May:* Sow a main-crop variety.
> *June:* When the plants begin to flower, give the soil a good soaking.
> *July/August:* Harvest as soon as ready. When harvesting is complete, pull up and compost the plants.

Potatoes

The potato is by far the most important and versatile vegetable. This crop is divided into two – early potatoes and main-crop (or late) potatoes. Main-crop potatoes are not really worth growing in a garden – there are difficult problems with slugs, soil-borne diseases and potato blight. Your ground is far better used for a more valuable crop. These comments do not apply to early, or 'new', potatoes. They spend so short a time in the soil that disease and pest problems are few. Few foods can compare with the taste of freshly dug new potatoes.

> **Note** The fruits that replace the flowers of potatoes look like small, green tomatoes. These are poisonous and should on no account be eaten.

Almost any soil will produce a crop of new potatoes. Potato scab disease is less likely in acid soils. This need not be a problem in neutral soil, as scabs are superficial and the flesh underneath is perfectly edible.

Potato virus diseases are endemic in this country and new potato 'seeds' should be purchased each year. Earliness and yield are increased by 'chitting' the seeds. This is done by standing the potatoes, in a single layer, on a tray with the eyes uppermost. Keep the tray in good light in a frost-free place, such as the windowsill of an unheated room.

Good early varieties:
'Marls Bard', 'Swift' and 'Rocket'.

Some of the developing tubers grow at or just below soil level. These are subject to sunlight and produce a green pigment that contains solanine – a dangerous poison. An important part of potato culture is to exclude light from the tubers to prevent this happening. 'Earthing up' by hoeing soil from between the rows to the base of the plants is the best way to achieve this. Close planting is sometimes advised but I find that this is not very successful. Growing under black polythene is another possibility; this does exclude the light but it also increases slug damage and I do not advise it.

January: Purchase seed potatoes of an early variety and 'chit' them.
March: Plant tubers, buds uppermost, with 5 cm (2 in) of soil above them in rows 60 cm (2 ft) apart. Allow 23 cm (9 in) between the tubers.
April/May: Draw soil over the shoots as they emerge – especially in frosty weather. Earth up into ridges. When frost is forecast, cover the foliage at night with two layers of fleece or other type of protection.
June: Water in dry weather. Harvest as required, sufficient only for immediate use.

Potatoes are a popular item at local shows. Tubers grown in garden soil almost always have blemishes. If you want to enter your potatoes in a show, grow them in buckets as described on pages 78 and 79.

Potatoes are harvested by digging up with a garden fork. You will avoid stabbing the tubers by pushing your fork into the soil at least 20 cm (8 in) from the plant.

Radish

Radish is quick and easy to grow, provided the weather is not hot and dry. Most varieties must be harvested when young; otherwise, they become hot and tough.

Light soils are the best for growing radish. Because the crop grows so quickly, all the nutrients must be in the soil when you sow. A small amount of dried blood raked in before sowing will enhance the yield. You must sow the seeds very thinly along the row. Thickly sown seeds produce a mass of leaves and the plants then run to seed before forming roots that are large enough to eat. Too much water produces leaves rather than roots. In dry weather restrict watering to 10 litres per square metre (2 gal/sq yd) once a week.

Good varieties:
'French Breakfast' and 'Cherry Belle'; winter variety: 'Black Spanish' (this variety can be left in the soil and harvested in winter).

March: Make your first sowing under cloches that have been in position for at least two weeks. Sow a few at a time in rows 15 cm (6 in) apart.
April to July: Sow summer varieties at three-week intervals. By mixing two varieties you will extend the harvest period. Pull the largest roots, as required.
Late July: Sow a winter variety.
December: Cover with cloches.

Runner beans

If you want to grow runner beans in growing-bags or containers, you should choose a dwarf variety. Climbing varieties of runner beans are best grown in the soil. To get a reasonable crop, you must have soil in which a large amount of organic matter has been mixed. Runner beans supply a large yield from a small area. Pick the beans regularly, as soon as they are ready, and be sure to pick all of them.

Possibly the best beans are produced from a second, later, sowing. Never let runner beans be exposed to frost.

Support canes, 2 m (6 ft) or more long, are best crossed and tied in their centres rather than near the top. This applies to a wigwam as well as to a row.

Good varieties:
'Red Rum' and 'Desiree'.

April: Sow seeds in individual pots or large Rootrainers filled with multipurpose compost.
May: Erect the supports. Harden off the plants. If growing direct in garden soil, sow two seeds by the base of each support.
June: If you are using greenhouse plants, plant one by each support. Leave a few supports for a later sowing. Set traps nearby for slugs.
July: Sow two seeds by each of the remaining supports. Harvest fully extended pods before the beans begin to swell. Harvest them every other day.
All summer: Apply water at the rate of 22 litres per sq m (4 gal/sq yd) twice a week in dry weather.

Note Do not save seeds from an F1 variety, because they will not breed true.

Shallots

Shallots have soil requirements similar to onions. They are grown in the same way as onion sets but shallots produce by division – each bulb divides into a dozen or more. Shallots are very hardy and can be planted outside at the end of December. Harvest when the tops begin to yellow – usually in July. Dry them off in the sunshine and store them on wire-bottomed trays – they keep even better than onions. Save a few choice bulbs to plant the following season.

Good variety:
'Springfield'.

March: Rake the soil to a medium tilth. Plant bulbs 10 cm (4 in) apart along rows 20 cm (8 in) apart. Leave the tip of the bulb just showing above the soil.
April to June: Keep the area weed-free by hand or very shallow hoeing.
July: Lift, dry and store.

Spinach

Harvesting summer spinach. Pick a large quantity, because spinach leaves reduce considerably during cooking.

Three different types of plants are used as spinach:
- true spinach – a hardy annual;
- spinach beet (perpetual spinach) – a type of beetroot that is a hardy biennial;
- New Zealand spinach – a sprawling half-hardy perennial.

Spinach requires a neutral to alkaline soil with a high humus content. As with other leaf crops, a dressing of nitrogenous fertiliser will enhance your yield.

True spinach

Good varieties:
'Medania' and 'Triathlon'.

March to June: Sow thinly along rows 30 cm (12 in) apart. Cover the seeds with multipurpose compost. Soon after germination thin the plants to leave one every 15 cm (6 in). Closer spacing will cause early bolting. For a continuous supply, make a repeat sowing every three weeks. Do not attempt to grow this spinach in hot, dry weather. Sowings after the height of the summer may succeed.

Spinach beet

Good variety:
'Perpetual Spinach'.

End of May: Sow thinly in drills 30 cm (12 in) apart.
June: Thin the seedlings to 75 cm (9 in) apart. Apply a top dressing of Nitro chalk or dried blood.
July onwards: Harvest leaves until the plants bolt.
Late July: Sow a crop for over-wintering. A harvest may be possible in winter, and this will be followed by an early spring harvest. Pull up spinach beet as soon as it runs to seed, because the stems then become woody and difficult to compost.

New Zealand spinach

(only one variety available)

May: Soak the seeds in water for 24 hours before sowing. Sow one 'seed' (contains several true seeds) per 12.5 cm (5 in) pot of multipurpose compost, and germinate in a propagator or on a windowsill. If more than a single (true) seed germinates, use pointed scissors to cut off all but one seedling at compost level.

June: Harden off and plant out after there is no further risk of frost. Space the plants 75 cm (30 in) apart.

July until first frost: Harvest the tips regularly to encourage additional growth. Leaves can also be used; these have more flavour than tips because they contain three times the amount of oxalic acid.

Swede

A swede is a type of turnip. It has a milder taste and is somewhat more hardy. If you sow it too early, flea-beetles destroy the young leaves, killing the seedlings. To prevent this, delay sowing until June and cover the area with fleece immediately after sowing. Remove the fleece when the plants are large enough for thinning.

Good variety:
'Marian'.

June: Sow seeds in your brassica plot: very thinly in rows 30 cm (1 ft) apart. Cover the area with fleece.

July: Thin the plants to 75 cm (9 in) apart. Control weeds.

August: Inspect for powdery mildew.

October to December: Harvest as required.

January: Lift and store (unnecessary in mild districts).

Note A better way to control flea-beetle is to raise plants individually in Rootrainers and transplant.

Turnip

Turnips mature very rapidly, producing a crop in about ten weeks. They are brassicas and should be grown in the same rotation as cabbage. Turnips are best when eaten young, so you should sow small quantities every three weeks.

Good variety:
'Milan Purple Top'.

April: Sow in rows 30 cm (12 in) apart. Thin seedlings to 10 cm (4 in) apart.

May to July: Control weeds. Sow every three weeks. Thin seedlings. Water sparingly in dry weather.

June to December: Harvest as required.

Chapter 8

Pest and Disease Control

A spray-free garden, planned with wildlife in mind, will have fewer pest problems than one in which chemicals are used. This is because the chemicals also kill some of the creatures that eat or parasitise the pests.

There are thousands of species living in and visiting a garden, and very few of them will ever become pests. A species only becomes a pest when its numbers increase to a level where it causes unacceptable damage. There is the odd exception – a single rabbit is unwelcome in most gardens.

A healthy plant can withstand the loss of a little leaf or sap. A few holes in the leaves indicate that some other creature is enjoying the garden as well as you. This creature will no doubt provide a meal for something else – in nature, few creatures die naturally; most live only until they are eaten!

Grow exotic plants by all means but also include some native species to support the wildlife. One example is *Limnanthes douglasii* (poached egg plant), which is an easy-to-grow annual that attracts hoverflies. A garden with a large number of different plants will have fewer pests than a garden where the owner specialises in one or two species. Nevertheless, lots of bio-diversity does not eliminate all pest problems. You will have to take action against some of them.

Many of our wild plants look well in the garden. This wild angelica gives structure, height and interest.

Increasing bio-diversity

Large gardens can have the luxury of a wildlife border. This one includes guelder rose, teasel and cardoon.

The two ivy varieties growing up a pole provide late flowers, ample shelter and nesting sites for birds and lots of spiders.

Two excellent wildlife plants – phacelia and buckwheat – look well in a flower border. These annuals flower within weeks of sowing and continue flowering for a long time. The flowers attract pollinating insects and the seeds are nutritious food for birds. You will find them listed among the 'green manures' in vegetable seed catalogues.

Water is essential to all forms of life, and one of the best ways to encourage wildlife is to construct a garden pond. There is no need to introduce water creatures – water beetles will fly in and take up residence. Dragonflies, May flies and other species will lay eggs that hatch into aquatic larvae. The all-important microscopic creatures will arrive on birds' beaks and feet or on plants you buy in. It is surprising how quickly a small volume of water becomes colonised and how much pleasure there is in observing the process. The main benefit is increasing the number of frogs and toads, which feed on slugs and insects. The best way to introduce these amphibians is to add a little spawn to the pond in spring. You should obtain this from a friend's pond, as collecting from the wild is unlawful.

Many brassicas, such as these calabrese (broccoli), will flower at the end of their useful life. Where possible, leave the plants to flower and supply food for insects.

Tip

When you start a new pond, quarantine all plants in buckets of water for two weeks or so. Before putting the plants into your pond, search with extreme care for blanket weed. If you see any thin green 'strings', return the plants to the supplier. If blanket weed gets into your pond, you will find it very difficult to eradicate.

Birds are very welcome visitors, and watching them is a constant source of pleasure – to say nothing about their song. Birds are so easy to attract that no garden should be without them. Water, food and shelter are easy to provide. Feed every day throughout the year. In addition to putting food on the bird table, scatter some on the ground. Dunnocks (hedge sparrows), chaffinches, yellowhammers and several others prefer to feed on the ground. Give only the amount they will eat by mid-afternoon. Bird tables and feeding places are a likely source of infection of various bird diseases. An occasional scrub and wash down with a garden disinfectant should prevent this. Cats sometimes take ground-feeding (and other) birds. An electronic cat scarer in the bird feed area will deter the cats but not the birds.

One of the most common birds – the wren – is very active; it is also reluctant to feed in open spaces. In cold winter weather a little grated cheese scattered under your shrubs will help wrens to survive.

Bird boxes must be checked each year and kept in good repair. Some boxes have hinged lids; these must be securely fixed, because squirrels, magpies and other predators will break into inadequate nest boxes a couple of days before the babies fly.

Birds readily peck apples on the trees and on the ground while ignoring the ones that are put out for them. Add a fat ball to the pin and make an artificial peck mark in the apple – this usually does the trick.

Face bird boxes towards the north, as sun on a box of nestlings can be disastrous. Birds collect hundreds of caterpillars on which to feed their young.

Soil in which seeds have just been sown is very attractive to next door's cat. Squash bottles, half full of water, will keep the cats off until the seeds germinate.

A bed of Chinese vegetables covered with fleece. Note that the cover is kept off the crop with short lengths of garden canes capped with old film containers. This is an ideal way to control most pests but is useless against slugs.

Measures to take against specific pests

The best methods of pest control are the ones that destroy the pest and no other creature. This rules out yellow sticky traps and almost all insecticides.

Below are listed the most common pests, in alphabetical order.

Aphids

Aphids have other names such as greenfly and blackfly. They feed by sticking their mouth parts into a plant and letting the sap flow to their stomachs. This gives them a surplus of sugar which is deposited on plant leaves. This deposit (honeydew) makes leaves sticky; in addition, a sooty fungus may grow in it and cover the leaves with a black mould.

There are many species of aphids, some of which feed on only one or two species of plant. That is why a lupin may be smothered in aphids while your other border plants are free of them.

Aphid numbers increase at an alarming rate: a single aphid could become a million in a month. Fortunately, not all survive – there are lots of natural controls. Aphids are nearly all females, which produce live young without mating. Some aphids

survive the winter as adults; others lay eggs in the autumn that hatch in the spring. A few have wings; these spread the problem to other plants.

Note If you see ants running around on some plants, it is almost certain that aphids are present. The ants feed on the honeydew that aphids secrete.

Control methods

- Keep a sharp lookout for colonies developing under the leaves and squash them between your finger and thumb.
- Direct a jet of water at aphid colonies, but take care not to damage the plant.
- Add a little soft soap to water and wash them off.
- Allow grass to grow and remain uncut at the bottom of a hedge or in an odd corner. This provides ground beetles with an over-wintering area. The beetles eat aphids and other pests as they arrive, or hatch out, in spring.
- If you decide to spray, use a systemic spray containing pirimicarb. When used as directed, pirimicarb is less likely than other sprays to kill the insect predators.
- Blackfly on broad beans is easily controlled by growing the crop very early in the season. You can achieve this by sowing under cloches or raising the plants under cover and transplanting.

Cabbage root fly

A Brussels sprout plant infested with cabbage root fly.

119

The cabbage root fly looks like a leggy housefly. It lays eggs at the base of brassica plants. The eggs hatch into larvae that feed on the brassica roots and lower stem. The fully fed larvae pupate in the soil. There are two generations each year and three generations in the warmer parts of the country. Badly infested transplants usually die; lighter infestations seriously reduce yields. The larvae of the autumn generation sometimes feed in the buttons of Brussels sprouts. The first attack of this pest occurs when hedge parsley is in flower.

Control methods

- Use transplants that have been grown in individual pots or Rootrainers.
- Cover new transplants with fleece and leave it in place for several weeks.
- Fit a circle of plastic sheet 20 cm (8 in) in diameter on the ground round each plant, making sure that it fits snugly to the stem. This interferes with egg laying and provides shelter for beetles and other predators.

Caterpillars

Caterpillars are the larvae of butterflies and moths. Each species has a favoured food plant. For example, the large white butterfly larva feeds on cabbages, wallflowers and stocks; the tomato moth feeds only on tomatoes; and so on. Cinnabar moth caterpillars feed on the poisonous weed ragwort. You can have much pleasure watching puss moth and other colourful caterpillars that are welcome to a few leaves.

Winter moth caterpillars feed on the leaves of fruit and other trees. Fitting grease bands round tree trunks in the autumn is one way to control them. A better method is to encourage bluetits. Regular feeding, and correctly placed nest boxes, is all that is needed.

Leaf-eating caterpillars that are causing too much damage are best controlled by picking them off by hand. It is better to 'hand pick' caterpillars when they are small. For biological control, use a spray containing the bacterium *Bacillus thuringensis* (BT). Any caterpillar that eats sprayed leaves consumes the bacteria, which cause a fatal disease. I would much sooner hand pick and accept some damage than use this spray.

Control methods

- Search for and squash the eggs.
- Hand pick caterpillars.
- Cover food crops with fleece or enviromesh.
- Spray with BT.
- Spray with pyrethrum.

Codling moth

A codling moth pheromone trap. All the insects caught on the sticky pad are male codling moths.

120

The codling moth lays an egg near an apple fruitlet. The larva emerges, enters through the calyx and feeds until it is fully grown. While inside the apple the larva is safe from sprays (and birds). This means that, to be effective, sprays must be timed to kill the adults as they lay, or the larvae before they enter the fruitlets.

Control methods

- Pheromone trap.
- Spray with insecticide in late May; repeat three weeks later.

A pheromone trap is the best control method. It contains a chemical that smells like a female and attracts the male moths. The males stick on a pad of non-drying glue and the females remain unfertilised. The trap needs to be in place from the middle of May until the first week of July.

Similar traps are available for *plum moth* and *pea moth*. The plum moth trap works very well. The pea moth trap is not effective, because pea moths usually mate before searching for peas on which to lay their eggs.

Earwigs

Earwig damage on cobaea leaves.

Straw-filled pots to trap earwigs.

Earwigs are brown insects up to 2.5 cm (1 in) long. They have long bodies with a pair of pincers at the rear end – curved in the male and straight in the female. Earwigs eat small insects such as aphids. They also feed on plant leaves and the buds of flowers such as dahlias. Earwigs hide during the day and emerge at night. They can fly but usually run when disturbed. The female lays a batch of eggs in the soil and stays with them until they hatch.

Control methods

- Conduct a torch-light inspection of damaged leaves to identify which pest is causing the damage. (Earwig damage is easily confused with that caused by vine weevils.)
- Set traps by filling plant pots with straw and tying them upside down on the plant. Empty the traps every morning on a hard surface and tread on the earwigs as they run away. You can usually buy small quantities of straw from pet shops.
- Reduce the number of possible hiding places to a minimum by keeping your garden tidy and taking such action as plugging the ends of bamboo canes with a sealant.

Mealy bug

The mealy bug is a small sap-feeding insect covered with a white secretion resembling flour. Mealy bugs feed in the leaf axils, and other hidden sites of house plants and greenhouse perennials. This makes them difficult to control. As well as weakening the plants through loss of sap, they produce honeydew in which black, sooty mould grows. The leaves of infested plants become sticky and black.

Control methods

- Apply a spray to the colonies with an artist's paint brush.
- Introduce a biological control organism (*Cryptolaemus*) into conservatories and greenhouses, but only if the temperature is likely to be constantly higher than 20°C (68°F).

Red spider mite

The first sign of red spider infestation is tiny yellow spots on the upper surface of young leaves. The mites are below, sucking out the contents of the plant cells. As the infestation builds up (this takes only a few days), mats of fine cobwebs cover the leaves with strands that form bridges from leaf to leaf. If your eyesight is good, you may be able to see mites crossing these bridges. Badly infested leaves become yellow and brittle.

The red spider mite is red only when it hibernates; at other times it is grey with two distinct spots on its abdomen. (You can see these with the aid of a hand lens.) The mites feed on the green pigment in the leaf and cause considerable damage to a wide range of plants in the greenhouse. Outside they are most troublesome on conifers, where they cause brown patches of dead foliage.

An adult lays around a hundred eggs, which hatch in two weeks or less, giving a very rapid rate of increase. When the days become shorter, the mites leave the plants and hibernate in cracks and crevices until the following year.

Note A slightly larger bright red mite is sometimes seen running around on the soil. These are harmless and you can ignore them.

Control methods

- Thoroughly disinfect the greenhouse during your autumn clean.
- Remove any likely hibernating places – the stem of a vine, for example. Rubbing this hard with a gloved hand will remove bark scales under which the mites may be hibernating.
- 'Mist' the plants with a fine water spray as often as possible, because high humidity reduces egg laying.
- At the first sign of damage, introduce the biological control mite, *Phytoseiulus*.

Slugs and snails

Slugs and snails are pests in most gardens because they feed on a wide range of plants. Leaves become skeletons and young plants may be completely destroyed. Slugs and snails hide during the daytime and emerge at night to feed.

Slugs and snails have both male and female sex organs; after mating, they both lay small clusters of translucent eggs in soil cavities. The young are like miniature adults. At first they feed on dead organic matter. Beetles and other soil creatures eat the slugs' eggs and the young slugs. In most gardens other natural predators such as the toad, hedgehog and thrush are too few in number to give adequate control.

The small black slugs that eat tulip bulbs and potatoes seldom come to the surface. This makes them harder to control, because fewer methods are available.

An effective slug trap that does not trap beetles.

Control methods

- A search by torch light on a mild damp night will provide a surprisingly large catch. They are excellent climbers so look up as well as down. You can kill your catch by dropping it into a container of salty water.
- A few hours before your torch-light search, sprinkle a circle of bran around the most susceptible plants. The slugs will be on the bran instead of the plants and your catch will be bigger.

- Traps containing a solution of half beer and half water attract and drown slugs. Some slug traps form pitfall traps that drown beetles and other helpful creatures. To prevent this, sink a cup into the soil with a centimetre of the rim protruding. Fill it with the beer-and-water solution and protect it from birds and rain with a large leaf or broken pot. Slugs will climb into these traps and drown but the beetles will not fall in.

Invert the peel of half grapefruits on the soil and remove the slugs every morning.

- Use a slug killer that is based on aluminium sulphate (which is safe for other creatures).
- Encourage toads and frogs with a garden pond (preferably without fish).
- Apply a solution containing nematodes. These nematodes are microscopic worms that enter the slug's body: the slug stops feeding, its mantle swells and the creature dies. A pack of six million is available by mail order. The price may seem expensive but it does keep an area slug-free for six weeks. If you are using nematodes to protect potatoes, apply them six weeks before harvest.

Using nematodes

Wash the contents of the Nemaslug pack into a bucket. Add 5 litres of water and stir briskly.

Add 1 litre of concentrate to a 10 litre can and stir.

Water the mixture over the soil by the plants that need protecting.

We are often advised to place a barrier of grit or crushed eggshells around vulnerable plants. I have never had much success with this method.

Vine weevil

Vine weevil larvae and adult vine weevil.

The vine weevil is a very troublesome and difficult pest. The adults cannot fly but they can certainly climb. They feed on plant leaves, giving them a distinct notched pattern around the edges. Although they feed on a wide range of plants, their favourites are tough evergreen leaves, including bergenia, camellia, rhododendron and ivies. The eggs are laid on the soil surface around the host plant. The larvae feed on the plant's roots, often taking the whole of the plant's root system. Many plants are chosen but preferred ones include sedums, fuchsias, primulas, begonias and strawberries. Plants in containers of soil-less compost are very susceptible to vine weevil.

Control methods

- A torch-light hunt to find the adults. You need to look carefully, because they fall to the ground and play dead.
- Water a 250:1 solution of Armillatox on the soil around susceptible plants once a week when the adults are active (look for the damaged leaves). This solution destroys eggs that the adults deposit in large numbers near the surface. Take care not to get any solution on the leaves.
- In spring, when preparing containers for planting young, grub-free plants, use your usual compost except for the top 5 cm (2 in). Use a compost that contains insecticide for the top layer. The eggs will be laid in this and the young grubs killed as they hatch.
- Water the broad-spectrum, systemic insecticide Pravado onto the compost. Use it with extreme care!
- In September apply the parasitic nematode *Heterorhabditis* on the compost around the plants you want to protect.

Whitefly (greenhouse)

The greenhouse whitefly is a different species from the brassica whitefly that is often seen on Brussels sprouts and other brassicas. Brassica whiteflies do not invade the greenhouse.

The greenhouse whitefly is a small (3 mm; 0.125 in) white flying insect that spends its time on the underside of plant leaves. When disturbed, it flies into the air. The eggs hatch into circular scale-like larvae; these stay in one place and suck the plant juices from the underside of the leaves. Whitefly-infested plants become covered in honey-dew and black sooty mould. In warm weather it takes only three weeks from egg to laying adult and the population increases at an alarming rate. A large range of food and ornamental plants is affected.

Whitefly eggs and scales are immune to available chemical sprays and so are many of the adults. Spraying whitefly is a complete waste of time and will do more harm than good.

The greenhouse whitefly is usually introduced as eggs or larvae on bought-in plants. It is possible that whitefly could travel from a nearby greenhouse.

Control methods

- Spray plants with soapy water, wetting the undersides of the leaves. The more often you do this, the more effective it will be.
- Suck up adults with a vacuum cleaner. But take care! Do not damage the plants.
- Use biological control – *Encarsia* (three introductions) for light infestations early in the year and *Delphastus* for heavy infestations. (Follow the instructions on the packet.)
- Growing marigolds in a greenhouse may prevent an infestation from starting, but I have seen many greenhouses with both marigolds and whitefly infestations.

Note Aphids shed a white skin that is sometimes mistaken for whitefly. The skins do not fly – the whitefly does.

Making it easier

In the conservatory, whitefly and mealy bug are extremely difficult to control. These pests are introduced on new plants. Before using any of the control methods mentioned above, you should consider throwing all the plants in the dustbin. Keep the conservatory plant-free for a couple of weeks and then start again; this time operate a strict quarantine as described on page 126. I know it seems dreadful to throw plants away but it is the most effective, and possibly the cheapest, method in the long run.

Biological control methods

Biological control involves the introduction of a predator, a parasite or a disease to reduce the number of pests to a level where any damage they cause is acceptable.

Most, but not all, biological control methods are used in greenhouses. A greenhouse is kind to plants but it is also kind to various pests. Pests that are absent, or uncommon, out of doors may thrive in a greenhouse. Whitefly, red spider mite, mealy bug and some scale insects can become a serious nuisance. A new greenhouse will not have any pests other than those, such as aphids, that already exist in the garden.

You are the most likely person to introduce new pests to the greenhouse or conservatory! New plants may harbour pests, or the eggs of pests. The best way to prevent accidental introduction is to grow as many of your plants as possible from seed. If you have to buy plants, place them in very large plastic bags and quarantine them for three weeks or so. After the quarantine period, inspect the plants, paying particular attention to the undersides of the leaves. After you have inspected the parts above the soil, remove the pot and examine the soil ball for any sign of vine weevil larvae, New Zealand flatworms or their black eggs.

Do not use yellow sticky traps, because they trap helpful parasites and predators as well as pests. Moreover, the yellow colour might attract winged pests that have flown from other greenhouses. Insecticidal sprays are useless against several greenhouse and garden pests. A few adults may be killed but seldom their eggs and larvae. There are effective sprays against greenfly but these may also kill helpful parasites and predators.

The most troublesome pests can be controlled (though not eliminated) by introducing biological control organisms. Biological control creatures are completely harmless to all but the target pest. They can also be used with confidence in a conservatory. Kew and other botanical gardens use biological control methods in their greenhouses.

If you don't use any insecticides, natural predators will thrive in the garden and greenhouse, controlling many of your pests. Predators include birds, frogs, toads, wasps, hoverfly, beetle, lacewing, and ladybird. Parasites will also be present; they are too small to be noticed but are very effective in reducing the number of pests.

Phytoseiulus *mites (left) introduced to control red spider mites. The pests are the smaller mites with two spots. This control method is also effective in the garden on conifers and runner beans.*
◀

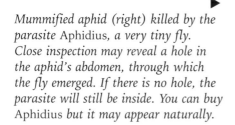

▶

Mummified aphid (right) killed by the parasite Aphidius, *a very tiny fly. Close inspection may reveal a hole in the aphid's abdomen, through which the fly emerged. If there is no hole, the parasite will still be inside. You can buy* Aphidius *but it may appear naturally.*

The red spider predators *Phytoseiulus* arrive in tubes of vermiculite. Warm the tube in your hand for a few minutes so the mites are active. Rotate the tube to mix the mites with the vermiculite. Scatter the tube contents on the infected leaves, catching spillage on a sheet of white paper. The tiny mites will be just visible on the paper; as they tend to walk upwards, lean the paper against the bottom of an infested plant. They will soon climb and begin feeding on the red spiders and their eggs.

Tap a little of the contents of the tube onto infested leaves, holding a paper underneath to catch spillages.

Using biological control methods

Organisms are sent by post and must be introduced as soon after arrival as possible. If delay is unavoidable, keep the unopened package in a refrigerator (not a deep freeze).

- Introduce control organisms as soon as you know the pest is present and the temperature is high enough (see the chart overleaf).

- You must not use any insecticides for four weeks before introducing the organisms.

- Remove any yellow sticky traps.

- Release the winged organisms under a 'bug blanket'.

- You will need a different organism for each pest.

- To control whitefly, make three introductions of *Encarsia* at two-week intervals.

- *Delphastus* should be used for heavy infestations of whitefly.

- Introduce control organisms before the pests become very numerous.

- Be sure that you have correctly identified the pest. For example, skins shed by aphids are often confused with whitefly. If they don't take off when disturbed, they are not whitefly.

There is a danger of winged biological control organisms flying out of the greenhouse as soon as they are released. A fleece 'bug blanket' will prevent this. Place the blanket over an infested plant and release the creatures under that. After a week or so the creatures will be established and you can remove the blanket.

Biological control methods

Pest	Control	How it works	Sold as	Minimum temperature
Aphids	*Aphidius*	An insect parasite of aphids	Aphidius	Night 10°C (50°F)
Caterpillars	*Bacillus thuringensis*	A bacterium that kills caterpillars	Dipel and BT	None
Fungus fly	*Hypoaspis*	A mite-predator of fungus fly larvae	Hypoaspis	Compost 12°C (54°F)
Mealy bug	*Cryptolaemus*	An insect (ladybird type) predator of mealy bugs	Cryptolaemus	Night 20°C (68°F)
Red spider mite	*Phytoseiulus*	A mite-predator of red spider mites	Phytoseiulus	Night 10°C (50°F)
Slug	*Phasmarhabditis*	A microscopic nematode (worm), a parasite that kills slugs	Slugsure	Soil 5°C (41°F)
Vine weevil	*Heterorhabditis*	A microscopic nematode (worm), a parasite of the weevil larvae	Grubsure	Soil 12°C (54°F)
Whitefly	*Delphastus*	An insect (ladybird type) predator of whitefly	Delphastus	Night 10°C (50°F)
	Encarsia	An insect parasite of whitefly larvae	Encarsia	Night 15°C (59°F)

Notes

- Use *Encarsia* where the number of whitefly is small and *Delphastus* for heavy infestations. *Cryptolaemus* is more suitable in a conservatory, as a greenhouse might be too cold for it at night. Greenhouse aphids are most troublesome during late winter, as they breed at lower temperatures than their natural predators. Squeeze aphid colonies between your finger and thumb or wash them off with water and soft soap.

- If all else fails, plants badly affected with aphids can be sprayed with pirimicarb. Take them into a shed or garage to spray them so that you don't kill any helpful creatures present in your greenhouse. Two days later, return the plants to the greenhouse.

Plant diseases

Plants are subject to disease, and a vigorous plant is more resistant to disease than one that is less so. To maintain good plant health it is important that you water and feed your greenhouse plants regularly. A small amount of seaweed extract added to the feed helps to maintain a plant's resistance to disease. Plants growing in soil also benefit from seaweed extract. The most common causes of plant diseases are fungus and viruses; very few are caused by bacteria.

Plant breeders have been successful in breeding varieties that are resistant to disease. You will have fewer problems if you select these varieties.

Fungus diseases

A fungus consists of fine threads, known as hyphae, that grow inside living or dead tissue. The hyphae feed on the plant, destroying it as they grow. Hyphae form growths on the surface, and these produce clouds of spores (the fungus equivalent of seeds) that float into the air.

Fungus diseases are particularly troublesome during the autumn. Control, rather than cure, is the best way to deal with plant diseases. Strict hygiene in your garden and greenhouse is the first step.

- Store your pots and trays well away from your plants in a shed or garage.

- Before storing them, wash used pots in water to which you have added a little garden disinfectant.

- Remove dead plant material before it has a chance to go mouldy.

- Take yellowing leaves off Brussels sprouts and other brassicas each week in winter.

- Avoid wounding plants: snap off the side shoots of tomatoes when they are small; if a side shoot becomes large, cut it off with clean, sharp secateurs.

- After cutting diseased plants, disinfect your secateurs before cutting the next plant.

- Remove any dead or diseased parts of plants by cutting back into healthy tissue.

- Finally, keep the foliage dry and the soil moist.

An annual clean-up in the autumn is an effective way to control disease. Remove frosted and other dead plants as soon as possible. Make sure that all dead plant material is composted. Empty the greenhouse completely and wash it inside and out with an Armillatox solution – 5 ml Armillatox per litre of water. This will kill fungus spores and remove green algae from the glass.

Fungus diseases thrive in still, damp air. In the garden avoid overcrowding your plants. Prune fruit trees and shrubs to keep the centre open for good air flow. In the greenhouse give maximum ventilation during the daytime, especially in the autumn. If all else fails, use a fungicide. Select a systemic one and use it sparingly.

The main diseases caused by fungus are damping off, mildews, rusts, moulds, rose black spot, potato blight, leaf spot, clubroot and apple scab. In addition, woody plants are susceptible to honey fungus.

Methods of control

- Strict garden hygiene helps to reduce the number of spores.
- Generous distances between plants gives good air circulation.
- When pruning fruit trees, keep the centre open to improve air flow.
- Good ventilation in the greenhouse, especially during the autumn.
- Crop rotation reduces soil-borne fungus diseases.
- Take care not to wound plants.
- Preventative spraying when the weather favours an outbreak (tomato and potato blight).
- Wholesale removal of infected plants.
- Grow resistant varieties.
- Avoid growing very susceptible plants such as hollyhocks (rust) or Michaelmas daisies (mildews).
- Spray infected plants with modern fungicides (but take care to read the label!).
- Use Bordeaux mixture and sulphur products – these are allowed in organic gardens.

Fungicides

A fungicide is a chemical that is toxic to fungus. Some are systemic – that is, they enter the body of the plant and move through its veins. Contact fungicides remain outside the plant and can also be used as a preventative. There are fewer fungicides on the market than insecticides. None is effective against the whole range of fungus diseases. Some may damage certain plants, so read the instructions with care. If you use a fungicide, choose a calm day and set the sprayer to produce a fine mist. Only dampen the plants; *never* wet leaves until they drip. Do not spray in full sun – especially in the greenhouse where the leaves may be scorched. Avoid getting any fungicide in the soil – a spadeful of healthy soil has miles of essential fungal hyphae. The following year use a fungicide with different active ingredients. This will help to prevent a disease from becoming resistant to the spray. Fungicides are sold under various trade names – the active ingredient is named on the container, usually in smaller print.

You can easily identify grey mould (*Botrytis*): the infected part of the plant becomes a fluffy grey and, when the disease is advanced, clouds of spores

Grey mould on a tomato stem. The fungus entered through a wound caused by leaf removal.

arise from the plant when it is disturbed. Grey mould grows on both dead and live plants of all types. It often enters a live plant through a wound and is very troublesome in the autumn, especially

Fungicides					
Fungicide	**Disease**				
	Apple scab	Grey mould	Powdery mildew	Rose black spot	Rust
Bordeaux mixture					+
Bupirimate with Triforine	+		+	+	+
Carbendazim	+	+	+	+	+
Mancozeb	+		+	+	+
Sulphur dust			+		

+ indicates that the product is effective against the disease.
Organic gardeners can use Bordeaux mixture, sulphur dust and mixtures of sulphur and fatty acids. None of the chemicals is effective against downy mildew.

Grey mould on a young brassica plant.

during damp weather. At that time of year plants are losing their vigour and succumb more easily. You can keep the number of spores to a minimum by good garden hygiene.

Powdery mildew on pea foliage

Damping off

Damping off of seedlings happens on the windowsill and in the greenhouse. Patches of seedlings fall flat and a fungus grows on them. The recommended spray – Cheshunt compound – is quite unnecessary. Control is achieved by using sterile pots and new compost, sowing seeds thinly and not over-wetting.

Black spot

Black spot on roses is a common fungus disease. There is no need for a photograph here, because every gardener knows the black spots on rose leaves – even the resistant varieties of roses show symptoms at the end of the season. In the spring, prune out stems showing signs of the fungus. Spray with a fungicide as soon as you have finished your spring pruning. Organic gardeners may use a fungicide based on copper or sulphur. Several applications are needed throughout the season. Remove and dispose of infected leaves, and rake up leaves as they fall.

Note Some rose treatments contain an insecticide as well as a fungicide. Planting a garlic clove by each rose is said to deter aphids.

Powdery mildew (there are many different species) appears first as a white, powdery coating on the upper surface of the oldest leaves. The leaves often yellow as the coating spreads to other parts of the plant. Remove and destroy affected leaves as soon as you see them. It is seldom necessary to spray powdery mildew, as the flowers are finishing or the crop is coming to an end before the fungus arrives. Research from Brazil suggests that a solution of nine parts water and one part milk is as effective as the chemical fungicides against powdery mildew.

Several fungus diseases, such as the rust on the broad bean leaf shown here, appear towards the end of the plant's useful life. It is a waste of time attempting to treat these diseases; pull up and remove the plants as soon as your harvest is complete.

Clubroot

Some fungus diseases are carried in the soil. The most common is clubroot, which causes large, wart-like growths on the roots of cabbages and related plants such as wallflowers. This interrupts their absorption of water and nutrients, reducing the size and vigour of the plants. Control is achieved by liming the soil every three years and practising crop rotation. Transplants, grown individually in pots or large Rootrainers, are less affected by the disease.

Virus diseases

Virus diseases have several symptoms: plants may be stunted or distorted or the leaves may develop yellow mosaic patterns. Some weeds carry virus diseases without being affected.

There is no cure for a virus disease but there are measures you can take to prevent them. In order to spread, a virus disease has to be carried from one plant to another. A virus can be carried through the air by aphids and other sap-sucking insects and through the soil by nematodes. Your hands and secateurs can also spread a virus from plant to plant.

A common virus disease in greenhouses is tomato mosaic. The leaves become a mottled colour of yellows and greens, and brown patches develop beneath the surface of the fruit while it is still green. It is thought that smoking in the greenhouse is the source of many infections.

A virus is responsible for the rolled leaves on these potatoes. The peach/potato aphid transmits several virus diseases of potato.

Control methods for virus diseases

- Remove infected plants as soon as you notice them.
- Control aphids and other sucking insects.
- Keep your hands and tools clean.
- Grow resistant varieties whenever these are available.
- Control weeds.
- Purchase certified potato seed every year – do not save your own.

132

Not all viruses are harmful. The attractive mottling on the leaves of this abutilon is caused by a virus. This is harmless and will not spread to other plants.

Other problems

Blossom end rot of tomatoes and peppers

A very common problem with tomatoes is a blackening of the fruit at the end furthest from the stem. This occurs when the plant cannot absorb sufficient calcium. This, in turn, is caused by insufficient watering and irregular feeding. Large beefsteak varieties are very susceptible but it is seldom seen on cherry tomatoes.

Control methods

- Water regularly and always give sufficient at each watering. (Note that growing-bag compost may seem very wet on the surface while being dust dry underneath.)
- Plant two plants per growing-bag instead of the usual three.
- Change your growing method to one that supplies more water, such as the Bulrush system (see p 30).
- Grow a variety with smaller fruit such as 'Sweet 100' or 'Gardener's Delight'.

Replant problems

Soil where there have been roses, strawberries or fruit trees is unsuitable to grow the same type of plant again. When such plants are removed, you must replace them with completely different types.

Weed-killer damage

The slightest amount of hormone weed-killer can have a dramatic effect on crop plants. Leaf blades narrow, new growth spirals and twists. Fruits may be deformed. Brassicas develop swellings (galls) on the stems.

Preventing weed-killer damage

- Never spray on a windy day.
- The first cut of grass after a lawn has been treated with a hormone weed-killer will contain the chemical. Make sure that you do not compost this – dispose of it well away from the garden.

Chapter 9

Recycling and Reusing

The garden provides lots of opportunities for recycling and reusing. Foremost in recycling is composting. Composting reduces the number of trips you make to the local tip, reduces the amount of material going to landfill and helps to keep down the Community Charge. Composting is not only environmentally friendly, it also improves your soil and enhances plant growth. Garden compost, mixed with soil, is broken down by millions of tiny creatures that convert it into plant food. Garden compost makes the soil hold more water and gives it a crumbly structure.

Garden compost

Pile garden rubbish in a heap and it will gradually turn into garden compost of a sort with no help from you. A compost bin is better than a pile, because it:

- looks neat and tidy;

- makes garden compost more quickly;

- makes better garden compost;

- retains heat long enough for the whole of the material to heat up;

- gets hot enough to kill off weed seeds;

- protects from rain.

As you so often leave the greenhouse with a handful of dead-heads, side shoots and other organic waste, it is a good idea to site your compost bin by the greenhouse door.

The best and quickest garden compost is made from fresh, green material mixed with older, drier material. During the summer many gardens produce lots of grass clippings and little else that is suitable for composting. If possible, buy some straw – you can probably get it at a pet shop. Straw mixed with the grass works wonders: rapid heating and no slimy mess. One small bale of straw will last the average garden all summer. If you cannot obtain any straw, use newspaper torn into strips (tear broadsheets from the top of the page and tabloids from the side).

Most organic matter is grist to the mill for compost making. Weeds, dead plants, unwanted plants or parts of plants. Also uncooked kitchen waste, old compost from pots and trays and small amounts of newspaper and straw. It is quite safe to include poisonous plants such as privet and the green parts of tomatoes.

The following materials should *not* be composted:

- lawn mowings following treatment with weed-killers;

- cooked foods;

- diseased plants;

Do not hide your compost bin behind the shed or in some other dark corner. Position it in the sunshine, as this helps to warm the garden compost and speed up the process.

- weeds with roots that grow again (eg nettles and bindweed);
- woody prunings (unless shredded);
- cabbage stalks;
- prunings with thorns;
- cat litter and dog droppings.

Tips

- Before starting, fork the soil where the bin is to stand.
- Begin with a layer of stemmy material.
- Place a piece of carpet directly on top of the garden compost, even if the bin has a lid.
- Add mixed material whenever possible.
- Build up in layers 15 cm (6 in) deep.
- Sprinkle a little dried blood (or Nitro chalk) over each layer.
- Sprinkle a little topsoil over each layer
- Shred woody prunings, conifer clippings and stemmy plants.
- Dampen dry material before putting it in the bin.
- If possible, fill the bin in one go – the contents will heat up quickly, sink and make room for more.

A lawn mower being used to shred hedge clippings.

Emptying, mixing and returning the material to the bin is sometimes advised to speed up decay and make more uniform garden compost. This is seldom worth the effort – it is better to wait a little longer.

Clippings from regularly trimmed hedges compost well when shredded. If you do not have a shredder, try spreading your hedge trimmings thinly on the lawn and running a rotary mower over them. They will be chopped and collected at the same time. The result is not as good as shredding but is a good second best.

Your garden compost will be ready in about three months – the material will be a dark colour, crumbly, have no smell and the original ingredients cannot be recognised. If it has a nasty smell, the likely reasons are that you have too much soft material, or the contents are too compact, or there is not enough air in it. Having too much soft material (eg too many grass clippings) can make it soggy.

If it takes much longer to convert (say, a year), this is probably because it is too cold or too dry or there is too much woody material in it. Don't worry if the material heats up quickly and then is almost cold two days later – the bacteria will still be working. You may find that there are lots of tiny flies when you open the bin; they are probably quite harmless, and their larvae will be helping to make the garden compost.

It can be difficult to empty the bin through the small door at the bottom. Most bins are cone shaped and bottomless, so just lift the bin off the garden compost. Some of the smaller bins don't have a bottom door at all, and you might find these easier to use.

Choosing a compost bin

Your first consideration is size. Will it fit the place you have in mind? Does the garden produce a lot of compostable material? 'Large' plastic bins hold around 300 litres (35 cu ft) and small ones around 200 litres (23 cu ft). A wooden cube may hold

600 litres or more; 1,000 litres (ie a cube in which the sides are one metre long) is an absolute maximum – larger sizes seal the middle and formation of garden compost becomes very slow. The volume of material reduces considerably during composting. Other points to consider include:

- A large lid makes filling very easy. Check how easy it is to open with one hand. Is it possible to have one hand full of weeds and open the bin with the other?

- A well-insulated bin makes better garden compost more quickly.

- A good-sized door at the bottom is very useful, as it allows the garden compost to be removed without having to move the fresher material above.

- A dark colour helps to absorb the sun's rays.

- Wood looks more natural than plastic.

Sieving freshly made garden compost is quite difficult with a standard garden riddle. Use chicken wire, cut a little larger than your wheelbarrow and stapled to two lengths of wood. Make sure that you bend all the cut ends of the wire over so they do not scratch you.

The tumbler composter is very popular and many gardeners are pleased with them. I disagree; they take a lot of space and, when half full, are difficult to turn. The lid catches rain (which may fill your shoe when you turn it!) and rotating the drum does not mix the material at all well.

Return the material remaining in the sieve to the bin for further composting.

Uses for garden compost

Good garden compost may look like the multipurpose compost from a garden centre but it is not the same. Garden compost is seldom suitable for sowing seeds or potting up. Use it in the following ways:

- As a mulch around border plants and trees. Late spring is a good time to cover the soil with a 7.5 cm (3 in) layer of garden compost. It helps to keep the soil moist, suppresses annual weeds and feeds countless soil organisms. These in turn convert the garden compost into humus and finally into plant food. The activities of soil creatures help to make the soil crumbly, aerated and fertile.

- Dug into the soil during traditional digging. When it is used in this way you should mix it with the soil and not dump it into the bottom of the trench.

- During the preparation of deep trenches to grow plants such as sweet peas and runner beans. Garden compost is most effective when it is mixed with the soil throughout the depth of the trench.

- Spread over raised beds in autumn. This protects the soil structure from damage by heavy rain. Worms will have pulled most of it into the soil by the following spring. Any that remains can be lightly forked into the surface or simply moved aside when sowing or planting.

- Mixed with an equal quantity of top soil, garden compost makes a good base for annual tubs. Put the mixture into the bottom of patio tubs, leaving around 20 cm (8 in) to be filled with multipurpose compost. **Note** that for permanent plantings in tubs, the whole tub should be filled with John Innes compost.

The wormery

A wormery converts kitchen waste into garden compost – not much, but very good.

There are several different kinds of wormeries, all of which work on the same principle. The base is filled with coir in which the worms live. They are fed with kitchen waste. Worm casts form the garden compost, which you remove periodically and then start the process off again.

Begin with a layer of moist coir and put the worms on top.

Add several small piles of different types of scraps and kitchen waste. Lay a cover directly on top and then replace the lid. Inspect daily, add more food and remove any that has gone mouldy – or that is not being eaten. The process is slow to start but speeds up as the number of worms increases. The wormery gradually fills up with a mass of garden compost at the bottom and the worms towards the top.

Success depends on:

- Having the wormery in the best position – not too hot and not too cold.

- Keeping the contents moist but not wet.

- Preventing the material from becoming too acid.

Two different wormeries.

The wormeries in the photograph are 'Tiger Worm Composter' and 'Can-o-Worms'. The worms are different and so is the harvesting method. 'Can-o-Worms' has a tap to draw off liquid, the other does not. The garden compost is better if there is no liquid, as all the nutrients stay in the compost. If liquid is produced, you can dilute it and use it as a plant food.

Garden compost is harvested from the 'Tiger Worm Composter' by removing the top layer, complete with worms, and transferring it to a new bin (provided). The material left in the old bin is garden compost. 'Can-o-Worms' consists of a stack of perforated trays. As one tray fills, the worms move up to the next, leaving worm-free garden compost in the tray beneath.

Both systems work well, provided the conditions are right. If the conditions are wrong, the worms soon die out. When kitchen waste is in short supply, you can add a little rabbit food to keep the worms fed.

Using rain water

A water diverter: rain water is diverted into the butt until it is full.

Water that falls on the roof can easily be intercepted and directed into a water butt. When the butt is full, the water flows into the soak-away. This prevents the tiresome business of butts overflowing.

Additional storage is obtained by connecting two or more water butts.

Some water butt taps run very slowly. Dipping your can into the top is fine but only when the butt is full. A better method is to have a large container under the tap and dip into that.

Water butts can become very smelly and need frequent cleaning with a garden disinfectant. A few crystals of potassium permanganate (obtainable at most chemists) added to the water will prevent this. Other products are available in garden centres.

Empty tomato trays from the supermarket make good storage for shallots, apples and other fruits.

Old compost bags are useful as rubbish bags. The inside of plastic compost bags is black and this allows several uses. Forming a well in the bottom of a hanging basket is one. Another is a 'tree mat' to control weeds around a newly planted shrub or tree.

The wooden handle from a broken tool makes a dibber. Old tights cut into strips make good plant ties.

Reusing old materials

There are several uses for old, leaky hose and other leftover material.

A length of hose slit down its length will prolong the life of this net by protecting the leading edge.

To protect the bark of a tree from chafing on a stake.

Protect gas cylinder piping from the sun.

If your wheelbarrow has a suitable edge, a bungee strap is a quick method of securing a load.

There must be many skate boards collecting dust in garden sheds. A skate board is a very useful way to move a heavy item around the garden.

I have already mentioned using newspaper as an additive to compost. You can also make it into 'pots'. This is much easier if you use a frame.

Newspaper 'pots' are ideal; just a week after this photograph was taken, a lot of roots were growing through the sides.

Newspaper pots

The frames fit both broadsheet and tabloid newspapers. Pop a felt-tip pen through the holes to mark the paper and join the marks.

Cut along the lines with a Stanley knife. If your grandchildren want to help, make sure they use scissors.

Place the frame over a plant tray. Pop two rolled-up paper strips into each hole.

When all the holes are filled, hold the pots down while you lift off the tray. The pots hold each other up as they spring into place. Fill them with compost and sow or plant.

Do you need a tool rack?

A length of waste water pipe makes a good tool rack.

Fix the pipe in a vice and cut a slit along one side of its length as far as the hacksaw allows.

Cut off a 5 cm (2 in) length of the sawn plastic for each tool.

Fit each piece into a vice and drill a small hole opposite the slit.

Fix them to a batten using a round-headed screw with a washer.

The tools are easily clipped in. I have been using this type of rack for over ten years and the plastic is still good.

You can make a very effective planter with leftover material.

Cardboard boxes were used to make this planter. You need two boxes. The length and width of the smaller box should be 15 cm (6 in) less than the larger box.

Making a planter

Mix one part cement, two parts of concreting sand (not bricklayer's sand) and one part fairly coarse damp peat substitute. Mix and add water, little by little, to form a paste that is workable but not too wet.

Put a 5 cm (2 in) layer of the mixture into the bottom of the larger box and place three evenly spaced corks to form drainage holes.

Put the smaller box inside with an even gap between the edges of the two.

Pack the mix into the gap between the boxes to a depth of 12 cm (5 in). Leave for at least a week to set and then remove the boxes.

Chip off any square corners. Brushing with a wire brush removes some of the peat substitute, giving the planter a rustic look.

Using old building materials

In most areas there is a demolition yard selling materials salvaged from old buildings that have been demolished. These contain a wealth of material for adding permanent structural features to a garden. Old chimney pots in gardens are quite common but there are plenty of other materials that you can use in interesting ways.

A length of rainwater pipe over a stake prevents the hose from damaging the plants.

A Staffordshire gardener has used old granite blocks to create the county's famous knot in her garden path.

Using Victorian ridge tiles

This semi-permanent feature is easily made from eight Victorian ridge tiles.

Arrange the tiles to form an eight-pointed star. Eight is the best number to use, as more or fewer tiles  do not make a regular pattern. Check with a spirit level and adjust as necessary.

 Fill with top soil. If your soil is clay, mix in some grit before filling.

Cover the soil with a woven black plastic. This not only controls the weeds, it also prevents earthworm casts from spoiling the decorative gravel that you will be adding.

Cover with a 2.5 cm (1 in) layer of decorative gravel.

Arrange the plants and draw back the gravel from each plant in turn. Place each plant  through a hole formed by cutting a cross through the plastic.

Most unused seeds will keep until the following year, provided they are kept dry and cool. A screw-top jar that contains a small amount of silica gel is an ideal way of keeping opened packets dry.

Chapter 10

Moving Home or Staying Put?

We tend to slow down as we become older. Things that we used to enjoy and take in our stride become more difficult and take longer to complete. This time of life may also be accompanied with the loss of a partner and all the problems that brings.

You could consider moving house. In some circumstances moving would make perfectly good sense – in others it would not.

All too often the need to maintain a garden is a reason (if not an excuse) for moving house. But moving house is not only a great personal upheaval, it is also very expensive.

If the garden is the main reason for your wanting to move house, you could make it easier to manage. Changes can be made that reduce the time and effort needed to maintain your garden. This could give you more years in a familiar home that has happy memories.

Throughout this book there are suggestions headed 'Making it easier'. Check through these and consider any that apply to your particular garden.

Maintaining a neat and tidy garden is a battle against nature. Now is the time to let nature take over with some degree of control. A garden of fading glory is full of interest and happy memories. As nature takes over, become a garden watcher rather than a garden doer and you will have many pleasant surprises. Make sure that you maintain a good sitting area (or areas) with easy access.

The possible changes to your garden discussed in the rest of this chapter are not intended to be completed in one massive operation. Ageing is normally a gradual process and changes to your garden should be gradual too.

'Leave it to become a wildflower garden' is something I have often heard. This is bad advice – a wildflower garden is extremely difficult to maintain. Weeds in the lawn are a different matter. Left untreated, a lawn will soon have birdsfoot trefoil, daisies, clover, selfheal and other interesting plants to give it a new and interesting dimension.

A rockery planted with saxifrage, aubrieta, rock rose, phlox and alyssum can be left. These plants will soon take over, producing carpets of flower in their season.

Sow self-seeding plants such as lady's mantle, hardy geraniums, foxglove, honesty, poached egg plant, verbascum, Welsh poppy, love in the mist

This lawn is cut regularly but receives no other attention. It has become a mass of clover, which is green all the year round and has flushes of flowers between cuts in summer.

and some campanulas. Use a light, long-handled hoe to chop out seedling weeds and any flowers you do not want. This is all the attention needed: no bending, no planting – just a glorious mass of form and colour. A jobbing gardener will soon remove the dead plants in late autumn.

Borders and lawns

Reducing the size of borders and increasing the size of the lawn(s) can make a real difference to the time and effort needed to look after your garden. Areas adjoining the lawn, normally used for bedding plants, can be raked over and sown with lawn seed. Island beds in lawns can be abandoned and replaced with grass.

What about mowing the lawn? The additional size of the lawn is unlikely to make a huge difference to the time needed to cut it. If you can manage to cut your own lawn, do it as often as possible – at least once a week. This will make the job very much easier and you can leave the grass box off after the first two mowings – no clippings to remove or make into compost.

If you are unable to mow the lawn yourself, there are many good contract mowers who will keep lawns cut and edged throughout the season. There are also the unscrupulous ones who may over-charge and be unreliable. Age Concern locally may be able to advise. You should be able to find their number in your telephone book (try the *Yellow Pages*, under 'Charities'), or ring their Information Line (see p 150). The *Yellow Pages* is also a good place to look for a contract gardener. Other places where gardeners advertise include shop windows and local newspapers.

For major clearance jobs, there could well be a voluntary group, such as the Scouts or Lions clubs, in your area that will be only too pleased to help. Your local Age Concern group may be able to advise you.

The maintenance of a mixed border requires a lot of effort and can be time consuming. Biennials and annuals need planting and removing each year. Herbaceous plants require staking in spring and cutting down in the autumn. There is also the occasional lifting, splitting and replanting. The plants that need least maintenance are small conifers and shrubs. They can be left to 'do their own thing' for years. If they become too tall, or begin to encroach on the lawn, they will need cutting back. This is not an annual job and is something that a jobbing gardener could easily do. Make sure that you know how much you will be charged before giving the go-ahead. There may also be a charge for taking the prunings away if this is necessary.

If a mixed border is taking too much effort and time, convert it to a shrubbery by replacing herbaceous and other plants with shrubs. This does not have to be done in one massive undertaking; plan the shrubbery and add the plants one or two at a time over a long period.

Roses in borders can also be left to 'do their own thing'. They will still flower freely and give lots of pleasure. You could arrange to have borders planted up with musk roses. These are excellent shrubs and need very little attention. The best varieties are 'Buff Beauty', 'Cornelia', 'Penelope', 'Felicia' and 'Moonlight'. A thick mulch of bark or a plastic membrane will remove the need for weeding in the early stages. On no account should you consider ground cover roses. Tall weeds grow through them and roses have thorns!

Another good trouble-free plant is a prostrate juniper. This will gradually take over an area, reducing the work to almost nil.

Montana clematis grow very big, becoming impossible to prune and difficult to remove. By far the best clematis to grow on an arch or trellis is *viticella* – it is free flowering all summer, is resistant to wilt and the only maintenance it requires is cutting back after flowering (no need to worry about what pruning group it belongs to).

Apart from planting two small pockets with bulbs and annuals, this border remained untouched for eight years. The border provides evergreen leaves all year, fresh new leaves in spring, and contrasting foliage and flowers in summer. It is a haven for birds and gives pleasure and privacy to the owner. The larger shrubs were cut back hard the autumn after this photograph was taken. The jobbing gardener also took away the prunings.

The lawn was cut back to allow the low-growing hebe in the foreground to spread. This is contrary to some of the advice given but is best in this situation. All possible solutions to a problem must be considered – it is obviously easier to remove a bit of the lawn than to cut this beautiful shrub.

The front garden

A front garden used for spring and summer displays takes quite a lot of time and involves a lot of bending. Such a garden can be converted to very low maintenance by covering it with a plastic membrane and planting a few shrubs through it. A 5 cm (2 in) layer of gravel completes the job and the result is not unattractive.

The costs involved with this type of conversion are minuscule when compared with the costs of moving home. You do not have to limit this idea to your front garden; there may be areas in other parts of the garden that are suitable.

This front garden requires very little maintenance.

Paths

It is important to keep paths weed-free and non-slip. A weed-killer such as Pathclear watered on twice a year is a very easy way to control weeds. This job is best done when the weeds are very small, because large dead weeds are unattractive.

Algae and ice are the main causes of slippery paths. Diluted Armillatox removes algae, and is easily applied with a watering can. Keep an airtight jar of rock salt in a handy place to melt any ice before you walk on a frosty path. Be careful, though! See page or spillage on planted areas will damage plants.

The greenhouse

A greenhouse needs daily attention in summer and can cause problems when you want to go on holiday. If the greenhouse is there, you may feel obliged to use it and find it a burden. If you do not use it, the sight of your empty greenhouse can make you feel low. If the greenhouse becomes a source of worry, it would make good sense to sell it. Make it a condition of sale that the purchaser also dismantles it!

Selling a greenhouse creates the problem of what to do with the area where it stood. If it had a concrete base, you could leave it as it is or use it to display some garden ornament or other. A soil base could become a lawn extension or a place to plant one or two shrubs that would need very little attention – especially if it is planted through a plastic membrane.

Fruit trees

Fruit trees take time and effort – mulching, thinning, spraying, pruning and so on. All this is necessary when you grow the trees for top-quality fruit and as a hobby. However, the trees will not die if you leave them untouched. They can be left to do their own thing, as they would in nature. They will flower in spring and produce fruit that can either be harvested or left for the birds and insects to enjoy. Neglected fruit trees can become a paradise for wildlife and a pleasure for you to observe.

Soft fruit canes and bushes thrive on neglect – forget pruning, mulching and the rest of it. A soft fruit 'jungle' is a real wildlife haven and you can still harvest some fruit while leaving the birds to take the rest.

Glossary

annual A plant that grows from seed, flowers and dies in one growing season

anther The male part of the flower that produces pollen

biennial A plant that grows from seed, flowers the following year and then dies

bolt Begin to flower before making normal vegetative growth

brassica Member of the cabbage family

broadcast Sowing seeds by scattering them over an area of soil

capillary matting A material with fine pores that soaks up water, used to water pot plants from the bottom.

compost Material that is used in pots and trays instead of soil

damping down Wetting the greenhouse floor

drill Shallow trench in which seeds are sown

fleece A non-woven plastic fabric that transmits light; used to protect plants

foliar spray Fertiliser absorbed by the leaves after being sprayed on

glyphosate A chemical weed-killer

green manure Crop grown for the purpose of digging into the soil

harden off Gradually acclimatise a greenhouse plant to outside conditions

hyphae Body of a fungus growing in its food source – normally invisible

lateral growth Stems that grow sideways from another stem

mulch A layer of material placed or spread on the soil surface

multipurpose compost Material that is used in pots and containers for sowing seeds, pricking out and potting up

node Place where the leaf joins the stem

perennial A plant that lives for several years

perlite A very light material consisting of hard crumbs that is used in some composts

pH Units by which the degree of acidity/alkalinity is measured

potting on Transferring a plant from a small pot to a larger one

potting up Transferring a seedling or a small plant to a plant pot

pricking out Transferring a seedling to a pot or tray

rhizome An underground stem

riddle A garden sieve

rose The fitting on a watering can spout to produce a spray

side shoot A shoot that arises in the leaf joint on a main stem

soft fruit Fruit that grows on bushes and herbaceous plants (eg strawberry)

stigma The female part of the flower that receives pollen

stock plant Plant kept for the purpose of producing cuttings

stool The roots and ground level parts of a plant

systemic (insecticide or fungicide) Chemical, absorbed by plants, that becomes distributed throughout the plant via its veins

tilth The crumbly structure of the soil surface

top dressing Applying a fertiliser by adding it to the soil surface around a plant

top fruit Fruit that grows on trees (eg apples)

truss Cluster of tomatoes attached to one point of a plant's stem

vermiculite Very light crumbly material used to cover seeds, made from an expanded rock

vine eyes closed metal hooks that screw into a fence or wall for securing plants – or the wires that support the plants

water stress Reduction in plant growth caused by too little water

Further reading

There are many gardening books. Some are lavishly illustrated with brilliant photographs and very nice to have around. Others are sold on the popularity of television presenters whose pictures appear on the front covers. There are also lots of special-interest gardening books. If you develop an interest in a single species, or in one aspect of gardening, a visit to the library should be a first step in deciding which books to use.

A good reference book is a very useful thing to have – I recommend the following:

Cassell's Encyclopedia of Gardening, published by Cassell, London (2000).

An excellent reference work on trees and shrubs is:

Hillier Gardener's Guide to Trees and Shrubs by John Kelly, published by David & Charles, Newton Abbot (1991).

For garden plants and flowers one of the following:

Reader's Digest New Encyclopedia of Garden Plants and Flowers edited by Peter McHoy, published by Reader's Digest, London (1997).

The Royal Horticultural Society New Encyclopedia of Plants and Flowers editor-in-chief Christopher Brickell, published by Dorling Kindersley, London (1999).

For selecting plants to fit your space or initially designing a garden:

Right Plant, Right Place by Nicola Ferguson, published by Pan Macmillan, London (1986).

For greenhouse enthusiasts:

The Complete Book of the Greenhouse by Ian G Walls, published by Ward Lock, London (1996).

For polytunnel enthusiasts:

Gardening Under Plastic by Bernard Salt, published by Batsford, London (1999).

For comprehensive information on garden pests and diseases:

The Royal Horticultural Society – Pests and Diseases by Pippa Greenwood and Andrew Halstead, published by Dorling Kindersley, London (1997).

Some useful addresses

Age Concern England
see the telephone book for your local group/organisation

Some Age Concern local groups/organisations have a 'befriending' scheme in which volunteers will help with gardening work.

Foundation
Bleaklow House
Howard Town Mills
Glossop
Derby SK13 8HT
Tel: 01457 891 909
Fax: 01457 869 361
Website: www.cel.co.uk/foundations

Co-ordinates home improvement agencies, and can advise about those in most areas of the country. Some agencies include schemes for handyman and gardening work.

Thrive
Geoffrey Udall Centre
Beech Hill
Reading RG7 2AT
Tel: 0118 988 5688
Fax: 0118 988 5677
E-mail: info@thrive.org.uk
Website: www.thrive.org.uk

A national charity to improve the lives of older or disabled people using gardening. Thrive advises individuals, their friends and families how to adapt their garden and find gardening tools and techniques that reflect their lifestyle. As well as a wide range of leaflets on easier ways of gardening, Thrive also has an easy gardening website: www.carryongardening.org.uk.

About Age Concern

Gardening in Retirement is one of a wide range of publications produced by Age Concern England, the National Council on Ageing. Age Concern cares about all older people and believes that later life should be fulfilling and enjoyable. For too many this is impossible. As the leading charitable movement in the UK concerned with ageing and older people, Age Concern finds effective ways to change that situation.

Where possible, we enable older people to solve problems themselves, providing as much or as little support as they need. Our network of 1,400 local groups and organisations, supported by 250,000 volunteers, provides community-based services such as lunch clubs, day centres and home visiting.

Nationally, we take a lead role in campaigning, parliamentary work, policy analysis, research, specialist information and advice provision, and publishing. Innovative programmes promote healthier lifestyles and provide older people with opportunities to give the experience of a lifetime back to their communities.

Age Concern is dependent on donations, covenants and legacies.

Age Concern England
1268 London Road
London SW16 4ER
Tel: 020 8765 7200
Fax: 020 8765 7211

Age Concern Scotland
113 Rose Street
Edinburgh EH2 3DT
Tel: 0131 220 3345
Fax: 0131 220 2779

Age Concern Cymru
4th Floor
1 Cathedral Road
Cardiff CF1 9SD
Tel: 029 2037 1566
Fax: 029 2039 9562

Age Concern Northern Ireland
3 Lower Crescent
Belfast BT7 1NR
Tel: 028 9032 5729
Fax: 028 9023 5497

Publications from Age Concern Books

Money matters

Your Rights: A guide to money benefits for older people
Sally West
Over the last 26 years, *Your Rights* has established itself as the clearest money benefits guide for older people. Updated annually, and written in jargon-free language, it has already helped more than 2.6 million people discover the full range of benefits available to them.

£4.50 0–86242–341–4

Using Your Home as Capital
Cecil Hinton
This best-selling book for home owners, which is updated annually, gives a detailed explanation of how to capitalise on the value of your home and obtain a regular additional income.

For more information, please contact Age Concern Books (see box).

General

Freezing Food on a Budget
Sara Lewis
Freezing food for use later means that you don't miss out on those supermarket bargains just because you don't have time to cook. It's a great saviour too if you can't get to the shops or don't feel like cooking.

£6.95 0–86242–207–8

Healthy Eating on a Budget
Sara Lewis and Dr Juliet Gray
Opening with a comprehensive introduction to achieving a nutritionally balanced diet, this book contains 100-plus closely costed recipes for the health-conscious cook, all of which are flagged up to show their nutritional values and calorie content. £6.95 0–86242–170–5

If you would like to order any of these titles, please write to the address below, enclosing a cheque or money order for the appropriate amount (plus £1.95 p&p) made payable to Age Concern England. Credit card orders may be made on 0870 44 22 044 (individuals) or 0870 44 22 120 (Age Concern federations, organisations and institutions), or fax 01626 323318.

Age Concern Books
PO Box 232
Newton Abbot
Devon TQ12 4XQ

Age Concern Information Line

Age Concern produces over 40 comprehensive factsheets designed to answer many of the questions older people – or those advising them – may have, on topics such as:

- finding and paying for residential and nursing home care,
- money benefits,
- finding help at home,
- legal affairs,
- making a will,
- help with heating,
- raising income from your home,
- transfer of assets.

Age Concern offers a factsheet subscription service that presents all the factsheets in a folder, together with regular updates throughout the year. The first year's subscription currently costs £70. Single copies, up to a maximum of five, are available free on receipt of an sae.

To order your FREE factsheet list, phone 0800 00 99 66 (a free call) or write to:
Age Concern
FREEPOST (SWB 30375)
Ashburton
Devon TQ13 7ZZ

Index

Index

Age Concern is dependent on donations, covenants and legacies.

Age Concern England
1268 London Road
London SW16 4ER
Tel: 020 8765 7200
Fax: 020 8765 7211

Age Concern Scotland
113 Rose Street
Edinburgh EH2 3DT
Tel: 0131 220 3345
Fax: 0131 220 2779

Age Concern Cymru
4th Floor
1 Cathedral Road
Cardiff CF1 9SD
Tel: 029 2037 1566
Fax: 029 2039 9562

Age Concern Northern Ireland
3 Lower Crescent
Belfast BT7 1NR
Tel: 028 9032 5729
Fax: 028 9023 5497

Publications from Age Concern Books

Money matters

Your Rights: A guide to money benefits for older people
Sally West
Over the last 26 years, *Your Rights* has established itself as the clearest money benefits guide for older people. Updated annually, and written in jargon-free language, it has already helped more than 2.6 million people discover the full range of benefits available to them.

£4.50 0–86242–341–4

Using Your Home as Capital
Cecil Hinton
This best-selling book for home owners, which is updated annually, gives a detailed explanation of how to capitalise on the value of your home and obtain a regular additional income.

For more information, please contact Age Concern Books (see box).

General

Freezing Food on a Budget
Sara Lewis
Freezing food for use later means that you don't miss out on those supermarket bargains just because you don't have time to cook. It's a great saviour too if you can't get to the shops or don't feel like cooking.

£6.95 0–86242–207–8

Healthy Eating on a Budget
Sara Lewis and Dr Juliet Gray
Opening with a comprehensive introduction to achieving a nutritionally balanced diet, this book contains 100-plus closely costed recipes for the health-conscious cook, all of which are flagged up to show their nutritional values and calorie content. £6.95 0–86242–170–5

If you would like to order any of these titles, please write to the address below, enclosing a cheque or money order for the appropriate amount (plus £1.95 p&p) made payable to Age Concern England. Credit card orders may be made on 0870 44 22 044 (individuals) or 0870 44 22 120 (Age Concern federations, organisations and institutions), or fax 01626 323318.

Age Concern Books
PO Box 232
Newton Abbot
Devon TQ12 4XQ

Age Concern Information Line

Age Concern produces over 40 comprehensive factsheets designed to answer many of the questions older people – or those advising them – may have, on topics such as:

- finding and paying for residential and nursing home care,
- money benefits,
- finding help at home,
- legal affairs,
- making a will,
- help with heating,
- raising income from your home,
- transfer of assets.

Age Concern offers a factsheet subscription service that presents all the factsheets in a folder, together with regular updates throughout the year. The first year's subscription currently costs £70. Single copies, up to a maximum of five, are available free on receipt of an sae.

To order your FREE factsheet list, phone 0800 00 99 66 (a free call) or write to:
Age Concern
FREEPOST (SWB 30375)
Ashburton
Devon TQ13 7ZZ